The Oakes Papers

The Collected Works

A Compilation of works by Corey T. Oakes, Min. N.L.

Volume 2

The Oakes Papers Volume 2

November 2015

By;

Corey T. Oakes, Minister of Natural Law

Table of Contents

Section 1: Scotland..4

    Discussion on the nationalism occurring in Scotland

    Cultural Roots of Nationalism within Scotland's History

    Final Thoughts on Scottish Nationalism

Section 2: International Affairs & Cultural Examinations........17

    Regional Statelessness

    Q & A on International Relations

    Excerpts from Treaty of Versailles

    Structural governance

    3 Favorite Concepts

    Foreign Policy

    The Palestinian examination

    Examination of class reversal in U.S

    Questions on Historical Case Law

Section 3: Other Discussions...70

    Smoking Cessation

    Feminism

    The Napoleon Issue

    Confucius

    Capital Punishment

    Prison Tattoos

    Andragogy

Section 1: Scotland

Discussion on Scottish Nationalism

In this issue, we will be examining one of the most beautiful and dynamic places on the planet today, Scotland. Why Scotland, one may well ask. For our purposes, the answer of nationalism will help to start our answer. The question came up about the current form of nationalism taking root in Scotland and why did I think it was so important to examine? This of course got my interest, as it raises a great many questions about Scotland, the United Kingdoms and the U.S. Questions about economy, trade and international affairs among others. Not to mention the issues associated with the sudden appearance of an independent Scotland. Therefore I did as any good researcher would; I began to research Scotland's unique form of nationalism.

I began my research into the why of the question, by looking at the reasons behind the nationalism in Scotland. This required me to look at the people of Scotland and their relative history of nationalism. Now of course there are a lot of popular versions of what the people of Scotland are; everything from the mythical and romantic highlander to the versions created by writers like Sir Walter

Scott and Robert Burns. I settled on looking into research in databases like ProQuest, as well as others. I chose these, as they offer the best way to find the information when combined with research done in the digital records of Scotland.

In doing so, I was able to find a cultural incentive toward being nationalistic. One could call it the preservation of a culture through a nationalistic process. In other words, the culture of Scotland has evolved in order to survive in a British world. Given that much of the culture was created from the ashes of former tribal kingdoms, it is no wonder that when England was set to attempt to absorb Scotland, Scotland turned to those cultural traditions which would help to preserve some separate identity. Hence, the nationalist tone that much of the more romantic image gives us. As I go into the separate areas of inquiry, it is important to note that while I may present this work in an informal tone, it is no way intended to make light of any of the historical, cultural or humanistic issues which took place throughout Scotland's history. In that examination much of what helped to shape Scotland's nationalism was quite serious and tragic and should never be taken lightly by anyone. Yet, does it explain the current trends in nationalism? I would answer that it does, as in the historical context the undercurrent would seem to be freedom at whatever cost may be necessary. Although it has many times led to a more conservative style and more recently a labor stance, it has still held that Scotland should be separate in oversight at the very least. In this way the historical context has helped to shape the ways in which that separation occurred.

In the early historical context the theme was two opposing sides, those of the Jacobite and those of the Unionist. In this fight much has been studied as far as the reasoning behind the conflict, as well as the political and economic reasoning for both sides. Both sides actually lend to the principle of nationalism, as they both fought to have the Scotland that they wanted. This may seem a bit out of sorts, as the Unionist movement was fighting to join the Union with England, as it was a more economically sound ideal during the period. The Jacobite Rebellion was really more of a third party movement to keep the countries separate under Scottish Kings following the ascension of William and Mary. The Jacobite's saw the Stuart line as the rightful heirs to the Scottish throne, which culminated at the tragedy of Culloden. While both of these movements had a legitimate reason for being, the Unionist movement would ultimately win out, as the impoverished Scots were eager for an improvement of their state. So how do these events tie into the nationalist themes of today?

Cultural Roots of Nationalism within Scotland's History

First let us examine the Unionist movement by looking at the gains and losses for Scotland in historical information. In 1700's Scotland the economy was desperate and the futures of many a Scot were hinged on whether a union would happen. In his book entitled; "How The Scots Invented the Modern World," Arthur Herman mentions the dramatic schism that had developed between the lowlands and their highland neighbors. This schism would divide not only the peoples of Scotland, but the ideas as well. Even the religious views differed by region, with largely Catholic in the Highlands and Presbyterian in the Lowlands. Then of course there were some significant people moving mountains, such as John Knox, James Buchanan and a flurry of others. Like Martin Luther, Knox's reformation was absolute and offered an expected consequence, more power to the people. This image harkened to the Declaration of Abroath and to the images of an independent, sovereign nation. Knox's reformation would also unite the people in ways that no other nation of the time could have. The Kirk system and the educating of Scotland would prove to be a double edged sword of progress. James Buchanan was also on the move and the relative literacy of Scotland was ripe for absorbing his ideas. All of these elements would come together to inadvertently create a nationalism that was unique to Scotland alone. However, they would soon export many of the key elements to most of the western world, which would help to create another aspect, the underdog aspect. Having exported such things as the educational elements, as well as the overwhelming exportation of people at the time, helped to create a sort of "soft-spot," for the Scottish story among nations such as; America, Australia and of course Canada. This exportation of Scottish ideals and self-determination, was not always done through ideal means, in fact many times it was through the forced movement of people. Policies such as the Highland Clearances which tore entire families from the Scottish fabric and sent them half way around the world, also helped to entrench the Scottish underdog story. This entrenchment would end up helping to create an almost international form of Scottish Nationalism.

In fact Scotland has become even more unique in this respect, as they have helped to create the world in which we live today, yet they are still unable to separate themselves from their southern neighbor. Therefore we must look at the reasons for this. In the history of Britain there are a great many historical points where scholars like to point out events that helped to create the colonial powerhouse that was Great Britain. Yet many if not most fail to recognize that Scotland's greatest achievement may not have been the historical milestones on the battlefields, nor the educational system, but its relative adaptability. It would seem that in every instance that I have found, where Scotland has been faced with perceived ruin or hardship that they have adapted. For example, during the period of the Union Scotland was not really viewed as the well-educated powerhouse that it is today. In fact it was not really seen as a desirable place to Europe. So, the Scots reinvented what it was to be Scottish. Expanding on the romantic ideals that Sir Walter Scott and Robert Burns had given the world and playing down the stories that Scotland was somehow a backward and savage place. Now this may not have been the first time that Scots had reinvented themselves and it certainly would not be the last either, but it does give us a small glimpse into their adaptability. In my own opinion, this is what helped to create the unique and seemingly pervasive Scottish version of Nationalism.

Final Thoughts on Scottish Nationalism

Although this is not a really in-depth examination of the Nationalism of Scotland, it does offer a glimpse into what I believe makes their particular version of Nationalism so important. Their ability to adapt to the changing world, in which we all live, is truly a testament to the Scottish people. This adaptive nature has also led the Scottish people to all the corners of the world. Where they have indelibly left their mark and helped to develop the world in which we live. Helping to set down the building blocks of western society in such ways as helping to institute the rule of law, or spreading the ideals of freedom and equality and of course, education. They have even continued to evolve and adapt to the changing environments in Britain itself. By continuing to develop into the people that they want to be, they are paving the way for new innovators and adapting to the changing global climates. Their adaptability is in my opinion, the most enduring thing about them. They are not locked into ideals which stop them from taking advantage of the resources available to them, nor are they eager to be stuck in the romanticized versions which they created. Instead they are forever changing to adapt to the world around them, seeming to do whatever it will require of them to remain Scots.

This then raises the question of; why have they not achieved their independence from Britain? Well there are great many reasons. In previous attempts they had not quite achieved a homogeneous desire to be free of the bonds with Britain. However, in the most recent attempt there was a homogeneous desire, as well as economic incentive, but the powers that be in Westminster made promises of more devolution. This appealed to many of the people who were on the fence about independence from Britain. Of course the promises were empty ones, as the historic speed at which the Westminster government attempted to withdraw the promised powers shocked Britain to its very core. This move by Westminster was just the beginning of many moves which would actually benefit the SNP and the independence movements. It helped to give the Scottish people one voice and put the nation on one side of the isle, after this move the people of Scotland were no longer divided on whether they should remain a part of Britain. In the next election cycle the people proved this by overwhelmingly voting with the SNP. This was an attempt by the people of Scotland to gain the power of a unified voice in Westminster. Those in Westminster would have other plans.

In the coming year Westminster would again and again push for laws and rules which alienated the Scottish MPs and thus, the Scottish people. In fact the government at Westminster would help to create a proverbial wedge between the Scottish Parliament and the Government of Westminster that Scotland could not have done better. With elements such as the English Laws, English Votes, the Tories in Westminster are beginning to advance an English separation from Scotland. This is a bit of a historical turn, as the sentiment towards independence begins to be shaped from areas outside of Scotland. This is crucial because the popular slogans for the anti-independence groups was; "Better together." However, the new moves toward others independent ideal and rules, leads to the same end, separation of Scotland and England.

This does not necessarily need to be the end of the United Kingdom, as it would still be beneficial for the separate kingdoms to work together to advance a collective agenda. To this end independence would simply act as an equalizer of sorts, by allowing each individual kingdom to rule and regulate itself, while still being able to come together on shared issues. The nationalism of Scotland is really no different than any individuals ideal of self-rule in that, every person wants to be in control of their own life and only gives up pieces of that control when it is beneficial for them to do so. The same can be said for Scotland, except they gave up control over parts of their lives in order to meet certain shared needs. Now those needs are no longer being met by the shared system, thus they should be allowed to control their own lives and deal with their own needs, without the help of a semi-colonial power attempting to keep that control from a distance.

Section 2: International Affairs & Cultural Examinations

Regional statelessness;

and its implications on the international communities.

The issues which I chose to examine and explain are those which have to do with regionalism as it refers to the issues of statelessness and the implications for which this progression has on the international community. For this I will be showing a five minute excerpt from a debate on Scottish Independence. My reason for this is that the implications concerning this referendum in Great Britain are not only of National concern, but have international implications as well. This translates as well to areas across Europe and into the world stage, as it begs the question; what would a more regional statelessness mean to the international relations community?

For my first example, I will show the example through the eyes of a Scottish National Party member, who eloquently states the important difference between more traditional forms of stateless groups attempting to create a state and the road that Scotland has chosen to take in reclaiming their sovereignty. This shows how one of the options for achieving this statehood, achieves a level of

18

legitimacy by using political and social means. While others become almost the exact opposite end of the spectrum by employing more traditional violence or military means to secure their statehood. Yet both have serious security issues associated with them. On the terror or violence end, we are left with a myriad of security concerns, everything from guerrilla warfare to autonomous groups with targeted attacks on political, or leadership groups, as well as criminal organizations. These can have even further consequences in the international arena, as they can have far reaching effects throughout the international community. With the globalization of the international system leading to more and more interdependence, we have to come to some kind of a consensus on the issues surrounding successive states and stateless groups, as these will be areas of major concern in the coming years. Scotland is representative of a precedent, as it will show us exactly how these issues can be dealt with on an international stage, even if they fail, they will still teach us the lessons. This will especially be true due to the security issues in particular, as the U.K. is a permanent member of the Security Council and if Scotland achieves independence, how will that member status be affected? This is of course only one part of it, as there are other major issues when we look at their independence and their relationship to the E.U. Examining how this transpires, will definitely help us to find some of the answers to security issues that may arise as a cause, but more importantly, it may give us a bloodless, less violent way to decide sovereignty issues in the future.

Corey

12 April 2014

Questions and Answers on International Relations 1

Q.1. What differences exist between IGOs and NGOs?

A. There are a great many similarities with both IGOs and NGOs, but the main differences are that IGOs are State funded and deal with above state level issues, whereas NGOs are private member organizations that also deal with many international issues, within both the national and international communities (Bach 2014). Intergovernmental Organizations have been traditionally for dealing with international security issues, which became abundantly clear following both world wars, thus they have sought to incorporate ideas of cooperation between governing parties in order to ensure peace. Also many of these organizations have become essential to the economics of most nations on the planet. For instance, the EU is an IGO which has been able to achieve a very interdependent economy across Europe. Therefore many of the security issues involving European countries become interdependent to a degree as well. NGOs are also heavily involved in many of these same aspects of international concern, but their main purposes seem to be the

Human Rights issues and keeping governing parties from being the only International oversight, as well as attempting to solve many of the issues which come along with this purpose. For instance, in my forum from week 5 I mentioned the NGO UNICORN, which is an Organization that works on issues concerning worker's rights, but also works on ending corruption activities both within business and governing bodies.

Q. 2. What does "The Tragedy of the Commons" refer to?

A. The Tragedy of the Commons refers to the problem of collective goods being depleted by overuse, thereby destroying the common areas which are all shared (Bach 2014). It was first articulated by author Garrett Hardin in 1968, where he proposed it as a description of the issues involved with overpopulation (Bach 2014). In the meaning of the tragedy referred to in the lesson, the parable can applied to many different areas of international concern, such as environmental concerns over the use and overuse of natural resources, or the economic stabilities of numerous actors in the international community. In fact with the interconnected nature of today's international community, it can virtually be applied to almost any issue, as many of our individual national needs have interconnected international applications and consequences. With the exploding populations in recent centuries, it will likely be applicable for some time.

Q. 3. What are Human Rights?

A. Human Rights as described in the lesson are rights which are applicable to all humans regardless of their nationality, religion, ethnicity or other individual characteristics (Bach 2014). They were described in many early writings as rights which are naturally endowed to man, or inherent in all men. This means that they are the rights to such things as life, freedom from oppression, or torture. In today's international environment human rights incorporate a great many more issues than these original meanings including, worker's rights, freedom of religion, equal treatment of the sexes, as well as equalization of many different cultural entities. It can be incorporated into many different aspects of the international community like International business, and International Health. In fact many of the NGOs and IGOs have human rights at the forefront of their agendas, sometimes even using human rights as reasoning for entering into an area where there is conflict, or obvious abuses of their conventions on Human Rights, such as is the case with most of their Peace Missions today (Cragg 2012). However, I would also like to point out that even though many of the Human Rights issues are beginning to be dealt with to some extent, without proper oversight and International Enforcement it will continue to be a rising issue (BBC 2014). This is due to the fact that without some kind of International consequence, there is little incentive for these violators to cease their activities. In fact, this seems to be an ever present problem in many of the issues in the International Community, not just in Human Rights, but International business, environmental concerns and many of the economic concerns too, it seems that without International Enforcement, there is little hope of these issues changing anytime soon.

Q. 4. Are you for or against Supranational Governance? Why?

A. In the lesson supranational governance is described as the move towards more international control and enforcement (Bach 2014). I would have to agree, as there has to be some kind of International Law that is genuinely enforceable. With the involvement of so many differing views on how we should do business, or even participate in governance in the international community, it only makes sense for us to have some kind of a structure to deal with violators of our cooperative agreements. If we fail to create some kind of oversight of these issues, they will continue to be violated. In other words, if we wish to preserve our environment, human rights, or security then there must be some way to make it work. I personally believe that giving the ICC more enforcement capabilities would only enhance its ability to create universal law that will benefit all of the international community. The trick then becomes getting super nationalist states, such as the U.S. and Russia, to give up some of their sovereignty to an International Court authority, not an easy task to say the least.

Q. 5. Do you connect more with economic nationalism, economic internationalism, or economic structuralism? Why?

A. I would have to say that I side more with economic internationalism, as there are many of the tools necessary to make this work, already in place. That being said, I would also have to say that I do not agree completely, as I believe that there must be a change in the state-run system due to the overwhelming international issues, many of which can be dealt with by many actors, not just states (Bach 2014). However, I also believe that groups such as the EU have shown that retaining some of the oversight at a national level can be beneficial to the overall European economy. I do not think that there is a strict adherence to just one of these theories, just as the different IR theories, one must incorporate many different aspects of each of these, meaning that in order to find a system that will actually work, we must combine these differing views to a degree, depending on the individual situation, much as the description by El-Erian when he talk about the three future scenarios of politics and economics in 2013 (El-Erian 2013). I believe that we as Nation-States can and do have the ability to create and implement the same principles that the IGOs and NGOs have concerning the economic structure, so long as we can agree. Therein lays the problem, as whether it is in a national sense, or an international sense, we will always have problems with implementation due to disagreements. Although this may be true, I do not believe that economic structuralism has neither the ability nor the presence to make that happen. In summary, I would have to say that I support economic internationalism with a bit of economic nationalism

thrown in for good measure.

November 30, 2013

Q & A: International Relations 2

Q. 2. How is Public Policy formed? How is the problem defined? Who is responsible for determining solutions, or setting the public policy agenda?

A. 2. As to how is, public policy formed, public policy is formed when a problem arises, or a change in the "normative" environment is changed. That being said let me explain the position, as the problem of a changing economy. Globalization is a term which encompasses a range of differing subjects such as, health concerns, trade, immigration and environmental concerns, just to name a few (Global). Yet, we cannot be expected to figure out who all is involved in all of these decisions as a whole, so we must decide on one. I have decided on an economic perspective to look at the globalization issue. As an economic issue, we can define the issues as those that have to do with outsourcing, trade, manufacturing, and of course environmental concerns. These issues are dealt with at many different levels, from the interest groups who have a vested interest in the outcome, to the Federal Trade Commission and the State Department. Of course there are a multitude of foreign interests involved as well, from foreign manufacturers of products, to the shipping companies bringing those goods to our shores.

As to the question of who is responsible for determining solutions, or setting the public policy agenda? I would have answer that, it is mostly the Executive branch who sets the foreign policy. However, more specifically it is usually the State Department who initiates the agreements with the foreign bodies. This is not always the case though, as many of the more recent policy changes have come about due to the actions of individual corporations, and their quest to get both their workers and their manufacturing processes cheaper, such as the case with Wal-Mart (Lesson 7). As the Global Policy Forum states;

"Trade agreements by the State Department such as, NAFTA and FTAA, have greatly facilitated the rates of international trade (Global).

When considering the globalization of the economy, we must also consider the special interest groups, as they are a very integral part of the globalization process. Consider the supermarket industry for example, with special interests in countries such as Brazil, Columbia and the Caribbean Islands. These even range from Coffee plantations, to small fruit and vegetable farmers shipping their goods to our markets. These are all going to have some effect on the overall policies in their respective countries, which of course will have an effect on the policies in our own country. This is largely due to the fact that, if we want to continue to compete at a global level, yet still enjoy our levels of comfort, then we have to give certain concessions to the other governing policies, to ensure competitive trade. The issues involved in the Globalization of the economy are much more vast than time would permit, so I have condensed it so as to save for space. It is my hope that this did not affect the information, or the explanation of it. If I have, then I apologize for any misunderstandings that I may have caused, as it is only my intention to inform.

25 April 2014

Q & A: International Relations 3

Q. 1. What is a network or Non-State Actor?

A. 1. There are many types of networks, but for our purposes we look to the groups which cannot otherwise be categorized into one of the other definitions. In other words a network is generally made up of a group or groups of individuals with a similar purpose and goal. In the week's lesson, they were described as groups with enough power to influence international relations, which are not NGOs, MNCs, or IGOs (Bach 2014). Many of these groups are made up of grassroots groups who actively advance their overall purpose or goals. These grassroots groups can either be of the civil persuasion, which would consist of groups such as, those in Bellingham Washington that banded together out of a loose agreement that they did not want to have coal trains moving through their town at all times, so they formed networks of individuals who were able to sway the local governing bodies into banning the transportation of coal through the city. This is a civil goal, gained through network activism from the area citizen population. An un-civil network is

something else, even though the basic structural components are the

same; the collective goals and purpose are of less than civil

intentions. These networks are described in the lesson, as groups

which have a destructive intention, or are of the anti-government

perspective, as well as those who belong to religious radical groups

otherwise known as terrorist groups (Bach 2014). There are of

course the other network groups which also can be considered un-

civil, such as the drug cartels, or loosely associated criminal

organizations (Arquilla 2007).

Q. 2. Why is Terrorism hard to define?

A. 2. Terrorism can be hard to define for many reasons, however the

main reasons are the agreements of the states on the definition itself,

taking into consideration the use of some of these groups by the

states as well. Taking into consideration the acts of violence, or use

of force used by governing groups throughout history, to either

replace or, sustain a political ideology. Not to mention there more

recent uses of what could be considered uncivil groups in state

sponsored war. I mean take for instance the fact that the colonial

Americans were considered terrorists by the crown. Taking the differing ideologies of the use of force to achieve an ideological or, political gain, into consideration is only part of it though, as the ways in which the goals are achieved is of critical importance as well (Bach 2014). The propensity to inflict fear in order to obtain an objective is also of contention, as it is precisely the acts of violence committed against those who are not the immediate target, but rather a means of instilling fear to coerce those in power into a particular action, which is one of the most accepted versions of terrorism (Bach 2014). At least some form of these characteristics, are generally found in most of the acceptable versions, thus one could argue that the definition of terrorism would then depend on who the people in power in a particular region are, as well as which of those is most beneficial to the international system as a whole. Not to mention that the advancing technology has created new networks of terrorist organizations that are completely different from the terrorists whom we are attempting to define today (Weimann 2010). Thus, it would seem that although the acts of terrorism seem to be rather easy to define, the definition of terrorism will probably be a target of disagreement for a long time to come. Well at least as long as there is no clear distinction between acceptable uses of force by groups to achieve a political goal and the illegitimate uses of force by groups to achieve a political goal, other than those decided upon by the actors in power at the time (Bach 2014). One good example of this distinction would be the beginning of the Iraq War, where the U.S. used a huge amount of force to instill fear into an entire nation's leadership, but was considered legitimate by the U.S. and their allies. I am sure that this was not the view of the Iraqi people, but again it was the viewpoint which differentiates the definition here.

Q. 3. Why do uncivil networks form?

A. 3. Uncivil networks form in opposition to an ideological stance, or in response to a criminal niche which may obtain a profit for the network groups involved (Arquilla 2007). For instance, the rise of Al-Qaeda, through the networks of anti-government groups in areas where the leadership has traditionally been brutal and militant, thus the groups themselves are also of a militant nature (Arquilla 2007). This is not always the case, as many of the new terrorist groups rising through mass communication tools, have been ideologically guided in order to better serve the anti-western sentiments, yet these groups may not really be as violently active within their perspective areas, they do help to spread the ideologies of their groomers, which does and has led to violent attacks on political targets through the use of terrorist tactics. Uncivil networks form mostly in this oppositional manner, yet some can also be created through state sponsorship, such as those in the tribal regions of Pakistan, early on these groups were utilized for their ability to fight a war which may have been difficult and expensive for the state. Once their usefulness was over, they turned to likeminded groups in the region to oppose the neighboring governmental bodies, as well as expanding the overall reach of the ideological basis, turning into radical versions (Kellogg 2010).

Q. 4. What is Human Trafficking?

A. 4. Human Trafficking is the profiting from or enslavement of human beings. The majority of which is truly the continuation of the slave trade, thus there are a few differing types of trafficking in humans. First there are those that are enslaved, kidnapped or otherwise forced into labor in mines, factories or some other for profit businesses (Kerry 2013). Then there are those who are kidnapped, forced or sold by family into the illegal sex trade, these are many times those of a younger age. Then there are those who are used for criminal activities, such as being coerced, or forced into drug smuggling, or forced to fight in war (Kerry 2013). This problem is prevalent throughout the world and has financial, physical, security implications in every area where it is found. The security concerns come from the profits and subversion of existing security measures. In the profit, they are contributing many times to uncivil networks thereby increasing the overall abilities of these groups to influence through terror. The subversion of existing security measures means that they are more able to penetrate target areas, which risks the lives and security of those who reside within these areas. This is also a huge violation of human rights, as these victims are subjected to varying types of abuses and tortures. It is a horrible violation of everything that it is to be human, free will, the right to life, but it also victimizes the many areas and nations in which it happens, as it also tends to be involved in many different types of criminal activity, thus it degrades the rule of Law, as well as threatening the economic and physical security of the populations that reside in these areas. No matter how this problem is viewed, it is

36

one of the most important issues to deal with as swiftly as possible, as it is an inter-related issue that is usually connected to many of the other security issues in the International community.

Q. 5. Why don't stronger arms control norms exist?

A. 5. Stronger arms control norms do not exist due to the legitimate use of arms for many civil actions, such as policing, security, as well as the military uses (Grillot 2011). For this among other legitimate reasons, it is hard to put control measures which restrict the use and sale of these arms. Then there are the oppositions of the actors involved in these sales, as the legal sales of these arms is in the billions, so one would be hard pressed to get any control that may limit this profit. This is also involving many countries, as well as the MNCs involved in the making and sales, as well as NGOs which fight to keep controls from being created (Grillot 2011). Therefore it would seem to me that if you are unable to come to any kind of unified set of controls for the arms, then you will never really be able to set up any kind of norms either. I say this due to the ways in which the competing uses of these very arms creates a sort of infinite cycle of violence, as having the arms makes those who do not have them feel as though they need them and when this occurs those who already had them will get more to defend against the perceived threat of everyone having guns. This perpetual cycle, combined with the nation building and securing uses of the small arms, creates an environment where there are no clear separations of the use, therefore how can there be separations for the control? Would not the situation be somewhat similar to the nuclear arms proliferation, as long as nations use these weapons for defense and policing, there will be those who use them for the very reason that their enemies have them. Then there are the contentions of trade, as these are both traded openly, as well as being smuggled (Grillot 2011). Thus, this too becomes an inter-related issue of trade, economy and crime. In the trade issue, we see that the illicit trade of any product will affect the cost of the similar products traded by an entity, in other words if a country is trading heavily in say bananas, but then the illicit trade of small arms is found to be also very heavily traded by the same country, then both the cost of bananas will go up, due to any trade embargos, or restrictions imposed by the international community. Not to mention, that if the bananas were on the shipping vessel that was seized due to trafficking in illegal guns, then those bananas will never make it to their intended destinations, costing the companies

that sell them, potentially huge sums of profit, as well as the losses

incurred by the consumers on the other end. This is of course only a

very slight examination into these issues and is not by any means

intended to be the entirety of these issues.

Excerpts from Versailles: The German Peoples Reaction

I have chosen to write about the animosity of the German peoples, during and after the Treaties of Versailles. There are a great many issues, which the German people were dealing with at this time, however, the stipulations contained within the Treaties, would send the German people into the arms of those who bring about the next wave of world aggressions. I will be attempting to show, that contained within some of these excerpts, are the seeds of discontent, which will lead the German People to create a sort of collective distrust of both their interim government, as well as the Allied and Associated Powers.

First, let us take a look at the conditions leading up to the Treaty of Versailles. To do this we must look to general consensus that the German people had, concerning WWI, a war that even though they were not the victors of, nor were they convinced that they had lost outright (2). This sort of collective delusion will come to be a condition which creates a view of the Allied and Associated Powers, as blaming Germany for a War which they did not feel responsible for. In our text, we see that this is a progression of events, not just some strange collective psyche, which materialized from nowhere.

In Chapter twenty five, it discusses the various effects that the war was having on the Home Fronts of the Countries involved, as we see the progression from the Pro-War sentiment, to the more severe conditions near the end of the war; we also see the rising tensions of the people at home. This eventually leads to the governments of the Central Powers, reaching out in despair for the olive branch of Peace, as this excerpt from Chapter 25 shows;

In the summer of 1917 the German Reichstag, made overtures to a "Peace of Understanding and Permanent reconciliation of peoples" (2).

This is the point where the Governing parties in Germany, decide to gain Peace, without which they would soon face utter defeat, but not all of the generals agreed, some even accused the politicians of being, "weak willed civilians" (2). These very generals knew that defeat was inevitable, yet they failed to admit it, instead choosing to blame the newly formed provisional government, for pretty much causing all of their woes, including admitting defeat. This delusional ideal of blaming others for their misfortunes begins to spread to the war weary people of Germany, as they watch their empire being given away and they are being billed for all of the destruction caused, they begin to resent this new found peace. By the time that the Treaty of Versailles is being negotiated, the collective psyche of this blaming has been quite cemented in the minds of the German peoples.

This brings us to the excerpts of The Treaty of Versailles (1). Where, certain Articles will definitely become articles of contention, for the German public. The first Article that I believe would have been a source of anger from the German people, would be; Article 116. This Article discusses the independence of the Former Russian Empire, as it was prior to the war, but it also has one part that is of particular disdain to the German peoples;

The Allied and Associated Powers formally reserve the Rights of Russia to obtain from Germany restitution and reparation based on the Principles of the present Treaty (1).

This would mean that the beleaguered German economy would have to somehow come up with ways to pay these reparations, instead of rebuilding the country, a contention which would stay with the German people for many years to come leading to many of them looking for something that would give them some relief from these supposedly overbearing policies.

This would not be the only Article which would cause a stir however. Article 119, would also be an article of contention, as it simply causes Germany to lose her overseas colonies (1). These colonies were a source of wealth and manpower, but they were also a source of goods, which the German people were in dire need of, in their post war state of despair. This article can also possibly be seen by the populace, as somehow adding insult to injury, as the country had already been virtually cut in half by the armistice, and now they were losing their overseas colonies as well.

The last Article which I will discuss is article 216(1). This particular article may seem quite simple and even somewhat ambiguous, but we must look a bit closer to see that it would not have been taken this way by the German people who lived in these areas. As this article the people of Germany are allowed to return to the areas where the armies of occupation are still located, but it has some provisions which would be particularly disturbing to the general populace. One of these is of course the stipulation that there return is; "Subject to the consent and control of the military authorities of the Allied and Associated armies of occupation" (1).

This combined with the facts of the war up to this point, would have possibly made the German people think that their entire world was being turned upside down. Many of them still believed that they were not really at fault for the war and thus, were not responsible for the rebuilding. The Treaty of Versailles may have seen the halting of the German expansion, but at what cost. Many of the articles contained within it, were too much for the population of Germany to cope with, which would eventually lead them to find ideologies which would promise the return of the Great German Nation, and relief from the seemingly oppressive policies of the post war Europe. I would even say that in the Treaty of Versailles; lay the seeds of contention that would lead to WWII.

An Examination of Structural Governance Issues

The level of analysis I am using for this examination is that of a structural analysis, as I am looking at the structural components of the UN-NGO relationship within the governance components of the international relations within the UN community. In this way I am able to showcase the future growth of such relationships and their implications on the global stage.

The UN is preparing for the future of International affairs by preparing to create an environment where the NGO's have less political affiliations and more involvement. They are attempting to keep these groups from undermining the states authority. This of course is not as easily achieved as many of these groups are set up to replace the state in many areas of global governance. The increasing technological communications advancements have created an environment where the states are seen as less effectual in creating solutions to world issues, therefore these NGO's have become the authority that the people of the international community have chosen to replace the states, as these groups have been able to solve many of the existing problems in the world. The UN has been working towards greater involvement by the NGO community, so as to have a more inclusive UN-NGO relationship going into the 21st century (UN 1999).

This begs the question, what will this further involvement mean to the states powers of authority? I would answer that it may undermine some of the authoritative powers of the states, but it may hold up the authoritative powers in some areas, as it could become the norm for the states too refer to the NGO powers on many of the more global issues, such as human rights. This will allow the states to relegate some of their more traditional forms of governance to other actors, in order to better serve the global community in the future.

If the trends of regionalization and statelessness continue then the degrees to which this amount of governance will likely grow as well, as many of the NGO's can better deal with the various groups within the affected areas than the states. This is largely due to the mistrust and cultural difference issues of many of these stateless groups, therefore if the NGO is not directly associated with the states authority, then they can be much more effective in resolving the issues associated with that group.

With this analysis in mind, it is my contention that as a global civil society develops, we will see many more NGO's taking over many of the roles which were traditionally associated solely with the nation-states. This could also be seen as a liberalist victory in that by becoming more involved in the system itself they help to create a more interdependent relationship with the states and the international community as whole.

The role of nation-states is changing as global civil society grows and becomes more robust. The needs of the United Nations and member states for partner-ship with civil society are increasing, but are not well defined. Demands on the UN system have increased in a time of decreasing availability of government resources for humanitarian and development assistance. NGOs are seeking greater access to arenas of policy and decisions making that have, to date, been the sole domain of member states. At the same time, NGOs recognize that their role with the United Nations is consultative. In recent decades, there has been a significant increase in the resources NGOs can direct toward technical assistance worldwide **(UN 1999).**

The nature and degree of NGO access to the United Nations have evolved in recent years. NGOs currently have three classifications of consultative status at the Economic and Social Council (ECOSOC). The accreditation system allows greater access for NGOs operating in more than one country. Access means different things: the right to circulate documents; access to informal preparatory meetings; observation and monitoring of various proceedings; the right to speak at meetings. Also, NGOs can be granted association with the Department of Public Information (DPI) which permits access, but not participation in UN meetings or deliberations. The United Nations also provides one-time NGO accreditation for a specific event such as a conference, which does not imply an ongoing affiliation **(UN 1999).**

26 June, 2014

Three Favorite Concepts

During this course I have delved into many different

concepts and ideas however, I would have to say that my three

favorite ones are; the systematic comparisons developed by the

author Tin Bor Hui (2004), the effects of globalization on the

international system, the effects of interventionism presented by

Fukuyama (1989). These are all to be examined under the structural

and individual levels of analysis. In this way I will be able to show

how they relate to international relations in a more effective way.

The systematic comparison of Europe and ancient China was

very helpful in figuring out the aspects of national interactions and

control mechanisms. Her comparison helped to show the relation

between the sovereign state governing bodies and their populace, as

well as how these relate to the international systems. By showing the

ancient Chinese methods of governance and inter-group relations to

one another, as they compare to the western system of inter-group

relations, the author was able to show how some of the

misconceptions in regards to these relations can help to cause these same misconceptions to continue. This was very integral to finding the correlates in the current international system, thereby avoiding many of these flaws in future examinations.

The effects of globalization are important to developing a current understanding of the international and inter-group relations in the 21st century. Kaufman shows some these effects and their consequences on the international system in his examination of the fragmentation and integration caused by globalization (1997). In it he shows how the effects of greater technological communications has caused many of the non-state actors to rise to answer many of the problems facing the world today, contrary to the recent past where the states had the monopoly on these effects. In the 21st century it is going to take many actors working across traditional borders to achieve the levels of positive interaction that will be required of the world community if we are to gain any kinds of lasting peace. These concepts then become paramount when examining solutions to many of the global and national issues facing the world in the future.

The end of history was a perfect title for this piece, as it really makes you think about the conceptual nature contained within (Fukuyama 1989). When thinking about the dramatic change in foreign policy of the United States, one does not really think about the interventionist policies created in the more recent past, but more of how the world relates to the ever changing nature of the regional issues involved with individual groups. However, if one looks to the end of the cold war, the notion then becomes clear in that many of the regional issues which have become major issues do have these qualities. For instance, the policies of the U.S. and Rwanda became the lack of interventionist policies became the inability to stop genocide. In the more recent past, there are the regional issues of the Middle East. In these issues the use of interventionist policy has led to the U.S. being involved in ever growing numbers of regional fights. Are these policies correct in their goals to equalize the human rights issues? I am sure that we will see, as these are fast becoming the foreign policies of choice.

These concepts are very useful in developing a working understanding of the current international concerns. I have enjoyed examining these concepts and have enjoyed the discussions regarding them. I am sure that these will remain current forms of interest, as these issues are very much involved in the everyday discussions of international affairs. The concepts of globalization, as well as the fragmentation of state systems of governance and the inclusion of non-state actors will continue to be a source of examination for the foreseeable future. The disintegration of these state systems will also continue to change the international systems and how they interact for years to come. The comparisons of systems will also be extremely helpful in the future as well, as it will give the insights necessary to develop a better world view in order to discuss and work out the issues that will inevitably face us in the near future. In short, all of these concepts will help one to develop a better view of the inter-group relationships that help to make up the international systems.

25 July, 2014

A General Examination of Foreign Policy

The global environment has a large part in shaping the foreign policy of the U.S. Just as the downturn in the American economy can have effects across the globe, so to do the events of the world effect foreign policy. For instance, according to Rosati and Scott the foreign policy of the U.S. during the cold war was to contain the spread of Communism [1]. As this was the case, events that took place internationally which were contrary to this ideology had effects on the foreign policy decisions of the time. In the 21st century we find that even more world events such as; economic fluctuations, international trade, upsets to governing bodies, the media and of course the people all effect foreign policy in some way, to what extent of course depends on the issue and whether it is an underlying issue that has no immediate effect on the U.S. itself, or whether like the attacks of 9/11, more immediate of a threat. The "Arab Spring" movements were a perfect example of how the structure of the global networks can be completely changed in the midst of a few months. After these movements began, the Middle East was the epicenter of that change, but by no means a contained environment.

Since the onset of the Cold War the system at first followed the patterns from WWII, where the President had most of the foreign policy power. This trend has reversed following the collapse of the Cold War on into the current period. [1]. However, with the events of 9/11 the President regained some of the previous foreign policy powers but even these are lessened comparatively. President Bill Clinton authorized U.S. actions in support of U.N. and NATO operations aimed at halting the fighting in the former territory of Yugoslavia, particularly in Bosnia. Under President Clinton, the United States participated in airlifts into Sarajevo, Bosnia, naval monitoring of sanctions, aerial enforcement of a "no-fly zone", and aerial enforcement of safe havens. In December 1995, President Clinton authorized the deployment of over 20,000 American combat troops to Bosnia as part of a NATO-led peacekeeping force to help enforce the Dayton peace accords aimed at resolving the Bosnian conflict. Subsequently, in December 1996, President Clinton agreed to provide up to 8,500 American ground troops to participate in a

NATO-led follow-on force in Bosnia termed the Stabilization Force (SFOR). These actions were taken by the President in the absence of express congressional approval, and despite continuing disputes between the Congress and the President over the proper course of action for the U.S. in the Bosnian conflict. Since then, the Congress has wrested more control over foreign policy issues. This helps to illustrate both the give and take over foreign policy points, as well as the continuing tradition of allowing the executive branch to begin foreign policy. Other changes which occurred during this period are the strengthening of a national security bureaucracy and the dominance of the global environment by the U.S., as well as the changes in the global economic environment.

According to Rosati and Scott, the roles of the President in foreign policy are; Commander and Chief, Chief Diplomat, Chief Administrator, Chief of State, Chief Legislator, voice of the people and Chief Judicial Officer [3]. As Commander and Chief the President has control over the Armed Forces of the United States, which has huge effects on how and what direction foreign policy will take. As the Chief Diplomat the President has the ability to negotiate agreements and to appoint ambassadors to foreign states. As the Chief Administrator the President has power over the executive bureaucracy which gives him influence over their activities and policies. As Chief of State the President has influence with foreign emissaries through the symbolism of the position. The President also affects foreign policy through judicial appointments, as well as the powers of veto in the legislative body and uses public opinion [3].

The limits and constraints on the fulfillment of the Presidents foreign policy are virtually the same ones used to achieve it. The sheer size and complexity of the executive bureaucracy and the intelligence community makes it extremely difficult to disseminate direct foreign policy goals. The largest constraint would probably be time, but the limits can also come from interest groups, or the people. Other constraints are of course Congress and the bureaucracy [3]. Another limiter could be the lack of credible information, or having information on a given situation in general. For instance much of the information generated by the intelligence community is taken from sources from various agencies and departments, as well as from more localized informational sources. It is then compiled and dissected by these varying entities, prior to being seen by those close to the policy decisions. Therefore the information must be verified and considered by a vast number of entities, so much so that it can sometimes be information which is no longer relevant. There are also outside constraints to consider, as these tend to restrict the President's options on foreign policy decisions to some degree.

Given what I have read, the Presidential action which I chose to showcase is the foreign policy decision made by George W. Bush to invade Iraq. Although the reasoning for invading Iraq was the possession of Weapons of Mass Destruction, none were ultimately found following Bush's Shock and Awe campaign [3]. Thus other members of the UN Security Council who opposed the invasion stepped up their opposition during the ensuing months following the invasion. This had detrimental effects on the outcome, as his approval ratings dropped, which of course gave other members of the governing body a chance to take back some of the power that he had managed to amass to the President's office. It also effected the actions that the President was able to take, as the opposition from the

Security Council and other actors domestically, forced the cabinet to

tread lightly so as not to do any further damage to the already

damaged Presidency [3].

March 14, 2013

The Palestinian Examination

Introduction

The Experience of the Palestinian-Americans is much the same as many of the groups that we have studied in this class. One significant difference is that the Palestinian Community has been unusually invisible to the American society, aside from times of great strife in the Middle East region. Their experiences as a community have been one of both success, and anonymity. Although Palestinian immigrants have been coming to America since before the Great Migration of African-Americans to the north, in which they managed to become a significant part of by trading with the burgeoning African-American community exclusively. This relationship has persisted to this day, allowing their enclave communities to grow stronger, both financially, as well in a sort of symbiotic assimilationism with their African-American neighbors.

The early immigrants did what many other minority groups before them had done, they created enclave communities. These communities were able to serve as a starting place for the new immigrants, as well as providing for jobs, religious security, and of course familial ties to their culture. These communities can also be used to help trace their relative cultural assimilation process, as many of these communities moved and evolved as general units, as they were able to gain more access to better jobs, and better overall situations. One of these enclave communities, which can be discussed in this manner, is the community in the Chicago area. Many of these respective communities were majority, or all male communities, and remained as such until the World War II. Many of these served honorably in the United States Armed Forces for both World War I, as well as in World War II (Chicago). Following World War II, many of these communities began to grow in earnest. The exact sizes of these communities however, is a subject of great debate, as most of these earlier immigrants were either classified as Jewish, or as simply white. This is a problem when trying to count these communities in the Palestinian groups in America. The Arab-American Institute Foundation estimates the number at somewhere around 250,000 Palestinians living in the United States as of 2008 (Ibish 2008). Another group puts the number slightly lower, at somewhere around 80 to 100,000 Palestinians living in the United States, in 2008 (Ibish 2008).

The groups living in the Chicago area have enjoyed a fairly low amount of institutional, or overt discrimination, this is partly due to their relative invisibility, as well as their similar looking physical characteristics. The Palestinian communities of the Chicago area also were not of the same religious ideology as the dominant culture in the area; however they were able to escape the majority of the negativity associated with this difference, by carving out niches in the larger African-American communities which they served. There was of course some hostility and discrimination though due to their relative position, in relation to Israel, and the lack of a state of their own. This is described below in an excerpt from the Encyclopedia of Chicago History;

> "Palestinian migration to Chicago, Muslim and Christian, has increased steadily since the late 1960's. It comprises largely of extended families from the West Bank, where Israeli military occupation since 1967 has stimulated extensive Palestinian emigration. A forced permanence was imposed on the Palestinian community of Chicago when Israeli laws denied residency and return rights to all Palestinians living outside the West Bank in 1967, as well as to those who subsequently remained outside of the area for more than three years"(Chicago).

This also helps to demonstrate a kind of Mirror Policy when it comes to policies that Israel has regarding the Palestinian community, and the policies that America has toward the Palestinian community. These so called mirror policies have historically followed Israel's lead, but as of recent years these have changed to some degree, as America is beginning to gear policies toward the Palestinian community in more of a unilateral approach. This means that America is beginning to side more with the international community in regards to the Palestinian community. The Mid-West region has long been a sort of safe haven for the Palestinian community, due in large part to the sheer size of the respective communities already there, many of which were able to escape much of the discrimination suffered by similar communities elsewhere. The sheer volumes of Palestinians communities in the Chicago area are described better by the Encyclopedia of Chicago History in this excerpt;

"By 1995 there were some 85,000 Palestinians in the Chicago Metropolitan Area; about half of these were born outside of the United States. Palestinians formed about sixty percent of the total Arab community in the Chicago Metropolitan Area" (Chicago).

This helps to show some of the major immigration from Palestine. I would now like to move to their respective assimilation issues. As many of the earlier immigrants from Palestine were classified as either of Jewish decent, or as white, we will look to the barriers involved with the communities that we do know.

Assimilation

The assimilation processes of the Palestinian immigrants, is much the same as other minority groups, in that they had to overcome language, religious and cultural barriers. The difference is that many of the early immigrants enjoyed a relatively mild set of barriers, including language, but the second and third waves of immigration had the enclave communities to assist them in both finding jobs as well as by helping with the language barrier (Carter). A study by Yinon Cohen and Andrea Tyree, describes these enclave communities in this way;

"The implications of such ethnic enclave communities have been studied for other immigrant groups in America. These implications are in reference to the propensity of second wave immigrants, tend to work for the first wave in enclave communities in Chicago, Detroit and other Mid-West Metropolitan Areas" (Cohen and Tyree 1994).

Other information on the enclave communities of the Palestinian community is; that around forty percent of Arab men are either professional, technical, or managerial workers (Cohen and Tyree 1994). Also, that nearly one of every two Palestinian workers in America engages in trade, compared to one in five among Israel, Jewish immigrants and the total American workforce (Cohen and Tyree 1994). This is also consistent with the other information gathered by the Cohen and Tyree study, as demonstrated in the following excerpt;

"Palestinian Arabs tend to own small businesses more than any immigrant group in America. Unlike Jewish immigrant businesses, however, most self-employed Palestinian immigrants in America flock into the grocery store business, where they appear to comprise a sizeable proportion of the stores in certain markets" (Cohen and Tyree 1994).

Also;

"....over half of the Self-employed Palestinians in the retail trade own grocery stores or restaurants" (Cohen and Tyree 1994).

This is also shown in a table from, "Diversity and Society", by Joseph F. Healey as shown below;

64

Group	Number	% Foreign Born	% That speak English >very well	% High School Degree or More	% College Degree or More	% of Families in Poverty	% in Managerial or Professional Occupations	Median Household Income
Non-Hispanic Whites	------	4.0	1.7	89.4	30.4	6.0	38.4	54,964

Arab	266,152	48.1	24.5	83.9	37.1	21.2	32.3	45,082
Egyptian	194,932	61.7	25.4	95.8	67.4	14.6	51.2	62,089
Iranian	413,845	64.5	27.9	93.3	60.1	8.3	54.2	67,919

Leban ese	489,3 64	22.5	7.8	91.8	45.8	7.5	46.1	63,495
Syrian s	150,5 27	23.8	11.1	91.3	40.2	7.0	45.9	55,461

(Healey 2010: Exhibit 9.5 384).

Many Palestinians have had relative success in the American society, not really encountering the usual barriers to assimilation; however, many of the Palestinian community do not see assimilation as a beneficial outcome. Instead many simply remain in the ethnic enclave communities, or they simply go back to the Middle East. In fact the large majority of Palestinians that immigrate to the United

States are sojourners, staying long enough to create some form of

wealth, and then returning to either the West Bank or Gaza. Of

course this generally only applies to those who are able to return,

according to the Jewish laws on residency, and return.

Conclusion

In conclusion, I would like to add that many of the

Palestinian community have been able to carve out niches among

many of our Minority groups in many of our major cities, and have

done so quite successfully. Despite their relative dispossession in the

Middle East, they have enjoyed relative peace in the United States,

and have even been able to become very successful members of both

our society, as well as the global community. As one source

describes their experiences, as unique among minorities in America,

as described below;

"They have been able to create Political Action Committees such as,
the Palestinian American Congress. In 2003 the American Task
Force on Palestine (ATFP), was formed to give voice to those
Palestinians living in the United States, who wished to speak for
themselves and express their support for an end to the conflict in the
Middle East. The task force is currently working on developing a
national coalition to support the two-state solution to the conflict,
which seeks to bring together Arab, Jewish and other American

Organizations which for whatever reason, support an end to the occupation and a life of peace and security for those who live side-by-side in Palestine and Israel" (Ibish 2008).

After 9/11, Palestinians received some discrimination, as did every Arab-American group. However, they were able to diffuse a lot of this discrimination through using comedy, and the local media to help solidify their position within United States society. Since that time there has been a great deal of reverence for the Palestinian community, as most of the prejudices and discrimination are directed at other more "physically recognizable" Arabs groups. In fact the majority of the discrimination and prejudice received by the Palestinians is due to their Muslim Faith. As with many of the dominant-Minority relations in the United States, they are ever evolving, however, the Palestinian community seems to be as adaptable as, or more adaptable than many of the prejudices which they face. Therefore, we will have to wait and see how the Palestinian communities deal with these prejudices, as they have always surprised us in the past.

Section 3: Other Discussions

29 July, 2015

An examination of the apparent reversal toward class inequality in the United States

In examining Jonothan Kozol's argument in his article on racial inequalities, correlations began to show up between many of the issues that the participants of his study were experiencing and their economic status. This led to the current examination of these correlations. The examination will be looking at the correlations by looking to different studies, as well as Kozol's study in order to see if there is further evidence that the trend towards a classless society has taken a reversal. This reversal is looking at the trend which began to some degree at the end of the Civil War. When reconstruction began the abolitionist movement strove to equalize the society to include African American citizens and was followed by many more equalizing movements all the way up to the Civil Rights movements of the 1960's. This was the trend towards equality. The evidence in this examination looks to an apparent trend towards inequality and classism in U.S. society. By looking to the evidence found in the following studies we will attempt to build an evidentiary road map, which will help to show the correlations between the evidence and the thesis that there is a trend reversal towards inequality among the classes. This will follow a traditional research examination style, as it will give the best explanation of the evidence shown.

Literature Review

Looking to the current trends in class differentials in the United States, it has become evident that there is a reversal towards a more classist society. The evidence seems to show the reversal occur the most in the fields of education and economic standings of the most neglected inner city environments. This examination has led to a great many different studies into this very theme. Six such sources will be used in this paper; some of these will be used more often than others, to ensure a good broad spectrum of information for the reader to discern their opinions from.

The first source that will be examined is called Class Action, which is a non-profit website dedicated to helping to develop an understanding of classism in the United States. It provides definitions for different types of class related questions. Although many of them are not exactly the same as the thesis, they are sufficient to show current views on the differentials, as they are viewed. This is the main reason for using the site as a source, to show some of the more modern evolutions of the ideas of class and how those are viewed by those in the United States in general. Thus allowing for a comparison view of how these views have changed over time by comparing them to earlier versions. It also helps to add to the evolution of class differentials in the United States, by showing current views of classism (Class, para 5).

The second source which will be examined is one which we are pretty familiar with, the article by Jonothan Kozol. This article helps to show how class differentials have affected the education system and the children in those areas. This not only will help to develop a more defined view of the ways in which our different social structures are affected by these class differentials, but will also lend valuable insight into the timeline of these class differentials and their effects. By looking to the unexpected results that the study produced and comparing those to the other sources, a timeline will begin to emerge that will show the reversal trends originally mentioned in Kozol's argument (Kozol).

The third source to be examined is a little different, as it was selected to show how the development of the educational materials and the lessons being taught which have evolved to fit with the evolution of the class differential ideology. This not only helps to develop the current sociological view of class differences in the culture of the United States, but also shows the levels to which the evolution has changed how these subjects are taught. Giving a larger picture to the structural differentials mentioned earlier in this paper. This will also help to add to the timeline of the class differentials (Myers).

The next source looks at the health differentials according to both class and race. The author looks also to the socioeconomic effects of the health differentials to show how they affect determinates to future health issues. This is invaluable in helping to describe the class differentials in a multifaceted and more holistic approach. By looking at this aspect of the structural class differences, combined with the other cultural and economic aspects from the other sources. A picture of reversal begins to take form, as the health issues associated with the differentials begin to show evidence of the results of those differentials. This will allow for the development of a much better class differential timeline, by helping to define the scope of the structural components (Nazroo).

The fifth source is one which helps to develop the early years of class differentials in the United States. He explores the development of the white superiority ideology in the United States through the 1800's. This really helps to show how the class differentials have evolved over time, yet remained none the less. It is sort of the beginning of the class differential timeline, as it shows the earliest ideas of clear classism. This can be compared to the current and recent past views of the class differentials to show the evolution of that ideology and how that relates to the classism existing in the U.S. today (Saxton).

The final source that will be discussed here is an article exploring the effects of class differentials on certain individuals from differing backgrounds. Even though it is only an interview and report type of exploration, it does help to show how the general populace views class in today's society. This lends to my other sources, as it helps to define the viewpoint of the current generations, as well as how the earlier ideologies have developed in the culture over time. This will also add a degree of depth to the sociological and cultural elements of my structural examination by offering a more broad view of the aspects, creating a more holistic viewpoint (Scott, Janny and David Leonhardt).

Overall the sources that have been shown here are all looking to the socioeconomic and racial differences that for some reason still separate us, even in twenty-first century United States. This is disconcerting to say the least, especially considering that one of the greatest American Ideals is that of upward mobility with hard work. These sources are by no means the entire story, but they do lend differing views of the same subject. Thereby, allowing for a more holistic approach to the class differentials. It is the goal of this study to show how these differing views can come together to show a picture of how the classism of the early American experience is beginning to make a resurgence in 21st century America. Then it can be expanded to create a more in-depth approach to solving the problem. If we as Americans cannot come together to fix a fundamental flaw in the structure of the fabric that binds us together, then what will bring us together? Should the people of the inner cities just accept the differences? By examining the causal effects of these issues, solutions can be found. The equality promised by the Constitution of this country has been neglected and needs to be revived, lest this nation be doomed to revert to a less democratic state. Studies such as this one will help to begin this process, by bringing the issues to the collective consciousness of the people. At least that is the goal.

Rhetorical Analysis

Jonothan Kozol's examination of the inequalities in the New York school system in reference to racial inequalities is concise and very informative. It also presents some unintended correlations, as it also lends some evidentiary information on the class gaps within these areas. Many in deeply economically deprived areas of the country are struggling to find ways to move out of their given situations. By looking at the racial segregation among the school systems in these areas, we are able to find solutions to help guide them out to some degree.

"In a Seattle neighborhood that I visited in 2002, for instance, where approximately half the families were Caucasian, 95 percent of students at the Thurgood Marshall Elementary School were black, Hispanic, Native American, or of Asian origin. An African-American teacher at the school told me—not with bitterness but wistfully—of seeing clusters of white parents and their children each morning on the corner of a street close to the school, waiting for a bus that took the children to a predominantly white school" (Kozol, Para; 6).

This is another way that Kozol's examination becomes more than a helpful article in a magazine. By helping to show the levels to which the trend of reversal has risen to, giving us the ability to examine the class differentials in these particular areas to increase our understandings of how the regional differentials correlate to the larger U.S. populations and class differentials.

Kozol conducts his study over a period of time and in a number of locations, which allows him an advantage in these traditionally closed societies. This gives Kozol a unique vantage point, as he is able to examine the environments as they interact, rather than through statistical analysis. This level of trust building also allows Kozol to interact as if he too were a part of the cultural group. Thus, he is privy to more of the actual information available to him through his interactions. So much so, that he is able to speak with children at the school and gets a real response. This is also crucial to my class differential examinations, as it helps to develop a structural understanding of the extreme end of the lower class differential. This gives us a sort of base line for which to look at the differentials in income, education and health care.

"High school students whom I talk with in deeply segregated neighborhoods and public schools seem far less circumspect than their elders and far more open in their willingness to confront these issues. "It's more like being hidden," said a fifteen-year-old girl named Isabel* I met some years ago in Harlem, in attempting to explain to me the ways in which she and her classmates understood the racial segregation of their neighborhoods and schools. "It's as if you have been put in a garage where, if they don't have room for something but aren't sure if they should throw it out, they put it there where they don't need to think of it again" (Kozol, Para; 12).

This situation is an opportunity to gather as much information with which to confront the systems faults, in order to remedy the inequalities that remain in these areas. Given the bleak outlook for most of these youth, we owe it to them to at least examine the issues and offer some form of remedy for the mistakes which still plague the people in these areas. It gives us a chance to own up to the mistakes of reverting to segregated and economic disparities. If we are to move in any kind of positive way, then we must first look to the areas where these disparities are the most apparent.

In examining the racial disparities in the educational systems, Kozol gives us the chance to understand the major class differentials which help to perpetuate the lack of economic upward mobility for the people living in these deprived regions of the United States. Many would argue that the racial segregation of the past is no more, but as Kozol has so eloquently showed us, this is not the case. With the poignant testimonies of the youth who live there and the admissions of those tasked with teaching them, Kozol is able to build an argument that is hard to counter. Using his collaborative efforts we are better able to understand the current trends and situations that these people are faced with on a regular basis. Thus, we are able to discern some very interesting fact about how the world views these areas and what the underlying structural factors are which continue these trends of separation.

"I asked her if she thought America truly did not "have room" for her or other children of her race. "Think of it this way," said a sixteen-year-old girl sitting beside her. "If people in New York woke up one day and learned that we were gone, that we had simply died or left for somewhere else, how would they feel?"

"How do you think they'd feel?" I asked.

"I think they'd he relieved," this very solemn girl replied" (Kozol, Para; 13).

Now we look to his purpose and what he was intending to prove and the results he was attempting to garner from his study. So what is his purpose? It is my contention that he was attempting to shine a light on the areas of our country that we probably wouldn't think about normally. The areas where he conducted his various studies are areas that most people in middle class America would never even know existed, as the media portrays them as dangerous lawless areas which have largely been turned over to gangs and crime with no real mention of the youth that have no choice but to live there. This sweep it under the rug mentality is another one of the many factors which help to perpetuate the reversals of segregated and economic disparities.

Kozol attempts to highlight the deeply segregated schools that still persist in the 21st century American culture. These highly segregated sections of the country have become segregated by many different mitigating factors. Many of which lead us back to economic disparities and there momentous progression forward despite the forward motion of much of the rest of the nation. His analyses of the structural and systematic forces which perpetuate the growing gap in education also lend themselves quite well to examining the growing class disparities as well. These include such factors such as sociological changes in the economic opportunities in these areas, or the great migrations of the industrial age. No matter the general causes of these disparities, they have also helped to create a rather significant class gap in the structural makeup of the areas in question. This is also compounded by continuing factors such as, the movement of students from more advantaged economic situations to schools outside of these districts. This only compounds the economic disparities of the youth and schools in the disadvantaged areas, as Kozol shows us in his rather explicit descriptions of the conditions of the schools in these areas and through the testimonies of the youth that live there, as well as much of the staff working in them.

"When I began to teach in 1969," the principal of an elementary school in the South Bronx reported to me, "every school had a full-time licensed art and music teacher and librarian." During the subsequent decades, he recalled, "I saw all of that destroyed."

(Kozol, Para; 21).

Kozol admits that even he was unprepared for the unintended factors which were revealed during his studies. In this we can see that while Kozol has developed a relationship with many of the schools and student in his study, he is also able to separate that relationship from the results of the study itself. We see this in his attempts to show the other factors arising in the study. He also is able to simply add them to the study by asking the participants if they have anything to add from personal experience. Many of these interviews are emotional and quite moving, but also help us to understand that this issue is not just a racial one, or even just an economic issue. It is actually a myriad of various factors which are all intertwined within a web of disparity, allowing for no upward mobility, or guarantee of a future.

This view becomes more and more of a mitigating issue in Kozol's study, as he tries to remain targeted on the structural issues associated within the educational disparities, yet he is hard pressed to do so, as many of the other factors continue to come up. This dynamic which is helped by his unique and trusted position within the given communities, gives him a unique opportunity to be the voice of these youth and he has no issue with telling his intended intelligent middle class audience of the factors which they may have some degree of control over. This is particularly evident in his repeated mentioning of the parents who choose to put their children into schools outside of their communities. As this is not something that the other families have choice in, yet the parents who choose to do this are actually taking economic support from the most fragile of school systems. While this may be a decision that is perpetuated by the lack of these schools to adequately educate their children combined with the fact that these are the parents who are able to afford to move their children, Kozol still sees this act as a sort of betrayal to the schools and the youth being taught in them.

Kozol gives us a view into a world which many of us would probably never even experience, giving us the ability to also see the structural disparities which threaten to return us to a time before the civil rights movements. If we are to change these disparities, then we must look to studies such as these. In his examination of the schools in which he was partially embedded, the sad truth begins to emerge that we are doing something that may be reversing the trend toward equality. Kozol even admits that chanting slogans and creating a more rigid educational structure in these areas will not work, nor will the slight upticks in testing data, nor will the introduction of positive message posters. All of these fixes fall short of the needs of the black, brown and poor, as Kozol puts it. What then are the summary results of his study? Well in his words, the best solution to the systematic reversion to segregated and underfunded systems is to return to the calls of the civil rights movements. Take up the banner of equality once again, shout and march against inequalities and demand that these areas be included in the supposed American dream. These are all given by Kozol as things we as a nation should be doing for not only ourselves, but for that little girl who wrote him stating that people in her neighborhood have nothing, while so many outside of these areas have so much. His study shows us not only the racial segregation in these areas, but also the appalling conditions which we as citizens are partially responsible for helping to create. So his results show us what we can do about it, instead of just sitting by and examining these areas as if we are examining some far off situation, we must instead look to these areas as they really are, our neighbors in need of our help. Kozol's examination of these areas does exactly that, it shows us that even one person becoming involved in these deprived areas can and will make significant changes to them.

Academic Argument

The evidence of how the racial and economic disparities among the inner cities of the United States given in these studies, is compelling. It offers a look into the structural differentials among educational institutions within these areas, as well as showing the unforeseen components of economic inequalities among the student populations. Yet is it compelling enough to say that it is empirical evidence of a reversal to a more classist society? The answer would of course be a mixture of yes and no, as it does offer evidence of a reversal, it cannot be applied to the society as a whole. This in no way should detract from the importance of the evidence provided, as the application to the society at large would be answered by further studies being performed in this area of inquiry.

For this study the evidence presented clearly offers insight into the class and racial differentials of the inner city environments. In this way the cause and effect questions can be answered in such a way that further studies can then build upon the information provided. So what are the structural differentials that seem to be pointing to a reversal to classism? For this answer one must begin by looking to the evidence provided in Kozol's study of the educational inequalities associated with racial segregation in the inner city environments where the studies were performed (Kozol 1).

In it Kozol looks at the differentials in education according to racial determinates.

"A teacher at P.S. 65 in the South Bronx once pointed out to me one of the two white children I had ever seen there" (Kozol 1).

By looking to these determining factors, Kozol inadvertently comes across some interesting correlations between the economic structures of the participants. This insight is where the correlation between the class differentials and racial segregation seem to become evident.

> "High school students whom I talk with in deeply segregated neighborhoods and public schools seem far less circumspect than their elders and far more open in their willingness to confront these issues" (Kozol 3).

This correlation creates a new set of differentials which lend themselves to a more classist version. This version allows us to look at the lives of the people who live in the inner city environments. By looking to the differentials presented by Kozol's argument, we can come to some conclusions as to the state of economic affairs, as they are described by the participants and statistical information presented. This allows us to build a picture of the differentials between the classes in these areas;

> "The dollars on both sides of the equation have increased since then, but the discrepancies between them have remained. The present per-pupil spending level in the New York City schools is $11,700, which may be compared with a per-pupil spending level in excess of $22,000 in the well-to-do suburban district of Manhasset, Long Island. The present New York City level is, indeed, almost exactly

what Manhasset spent per pupil eighteen years ago, in 1987, when that sum of money bought a great deal more in services and salaries than it can buy today. In dollars adjusted for inflation, New York City has not yet caught up to where its wealthiest suburbs were a quarter-century ago" (Kozol, Para; 27).

By building these class differential pictures to describe the issue of a reversal, we can see that there are many factors which help to contribute to the reversal. In the economic and racial descriptions given by Kozol and his participants we begin to develop a picture which shows that the detrimental situation that these particular schools are in is largely due to the unintentional separation of students according to economic situations. Following this up with information from James Nazroo's study of the inequalities in health care, we are able to build on this picture to develop a larger picture of how classism is reversing.

James Nazroo attempts to explain the socioeconomic effect on minority health. In his examinations into whether or not the socioeconomic factor could be factored out, he comes to the conclusion that it cannot, as we see in this statement;

"Overall, then, the impression is that across ethnic groups, across countries, and across outcomes, socioeconomic factors contribute to ethnic inequalities in health" (Nazroo 3).

An examination into the socioeconomic status of an individual and their prospective health reveals some very telling marks. The information presented helps us to develop the larger picture that the individuals living at the lower end of the socioeconomic ladder are far less able to gain access to health care. Building on the information from Kozol's argument, we can begin to see that the differentials associated with the lower socioeconomic status, seem to be prevalent in education, healthcare, as well as living standards. So how does this compare to the more current understandings of class in the U.S.?

Well, according to the website on classism in the United States, it conforms quite well. According to them the differentials in class are indeed real and very much a deciding factor in whether an individual has opportunities available to them.

"In our definition of class, poverty is more than an economic measure. True poverty is both an economic status and a lack of power over the forces in one's life. There are people who are deeply disenfranchised from society and have little power in their lives, even though they might have an income over the official poverty line. There are those who might be economically poor but are self-sufficient in terms of growing food or exercising power in their lives and in their communities" (Class, Para; 11).

This helps us to see that the view of class difference is quite alive and well in the 21st century, as are the widening gaps between these levels of access to upward mobility. It also helps us to develop a more involved picture of the class differentials in the United States, by helping to add to the pictures developed by Kozol and Nazroo.

These studies are by no means the entirety of the studies which need to be performed, but they do give us a place to begin. Obviously more studies into the outlying factors such as, criminal involvement statistics, or gender biases. Yet these studies do help us to see how the class differences in the United States have begun to revert back to their earlier states and if we are to halt these to any degree, then we must act. In looking to the class differentials given by these studies, we are better able to examine the reasons for the widening gaps. They may sometimes be out of our immediate control, but as we have seen in these studies, there are areas where we can intercede to insure a brighter future for our children. If we ignore the widening gaps, then we are doomed to continue to make the same mistakes as our predecessors. Given that the majority of the population in the United States lives in the lower 99 percent, the widening of the socioeconomic status should be disconcerting to us all.

November 30, 2013

Questions on Historical Case Law

Q.1. Choose a case from Lesson 5, then define it, and describe it then explain the impact of that decision on the American public.

A.1. I chose to look at the case of the Cherokee Nation v. State of Georgia, from 1831. The reason that I chose this particular case is that I read about this case when I was younger and I found it to be very crucial to the development of the United States that we recognize today. The basic facts of this case are that the Cherokee Nation brought the matter before the court to seek an injunction. They sought an injunction to restrain the State of Georgia from the execution of certain laws, which it was alleged, went directly to the annihilation of the Cherokee Peoples as a political entity (Marshall). It was also alleged that the State of Georgia was attempting to seize the land which the Cherokee Nations occupied, for their own use (Marshall). The court decides to perform an inquiry, prior to hearing the case. In this subsequent inquiry, they found that the State of Georgia being a party in the action, did give the court jurisdiction.

However, at the same time, the court found that the Cherokee Nation did not represent a foreign state and therefore, the court did not have jurisdiction due to the fact of the Cherokee Nation not being able to bring a suit because they were not a foreign nation (Marshall). They found instead that the Cherokee Nation was actually more of a dependent nation, under the care and protection of the United States (Marshall).

This decision was important due to the long term affects that it had. Another reason that it became a very important case was that it decided the fate of the relationship between the United States and the Indigenous peoples of the America. For the first time, there were no more treaties, just the rule of law, giving the United States supreme control over the lands from coast to coast as well as the rights to minerals and resources contained within that land. It also gave the United States parameters for future dealings with the Native American Tribes, as it gave them sovereignty over the tribes, but also the responsibility to protect them and help to support and educate them. This would be a huge contention in the years to come, especially during the 1970's, when the American Indian Movement would challenge not just the rights of the treaties, but also this very ruling. Although they may not have been overly successful in their taking of Alcatraz, or other successive movements, they were able to effect the ways in which they fought for their rights under the Constitution of the United States. Although this precedent has stood the test of time, it has also lent itself to many of the arguments for educational resources, energy usage, as well as a whole host of support issues in the years to come. As I am sure that this ruling, as well as the dissenting opinions, will continue to be of great importance for the sovereignty of the Native American Tribes for the foreseeable future.

November 2, 2013

An Examine of Smoking Cessation

It seems that Smokers' who have higher addiction rates, are able to quit at the same rate as smokers' with less addiction rates. Stopping smoking cigarettes is a daunting task for anyone who smokes, especially when their level of addiction is high. There are numerous studies which address this topic, yet many are more concerned with the effects on people's health, not with the difficulty of smoking cessation in general. Therefore, the studies which were chosen for this essay are ones which are aimed more at the examination of the difficulties associated with smoking cessation in adults. The goal here is to find the factors which are helpful to adult smokers who are also on the high end of the addiction scale. The example for scale is; smokers who smoke more than fifteen cigarettes in a day, for more than one year. The reason using this example is that, it helps to narrow the scope of the examination.

The first study examined was found in the ProQuest database, it was used for its relevance to the above stated subject matter. It was also chosen for its examination of the "Quitting Continuum" (Pierce 1). In this study they used a random sample survey of over 3,000 residents of California; they then followed up with these same respondents, five years later (Pierce 1). In the follow up survey, they asked questions geared toward finding out how far they had come in their smoking cessation, in the last five years. What they found was that; those with higher levels of addiction (>15 per day), had moved only one level up, or down the quitting continuum (Pierce 3). What they also found was that this group could also be separated into more groups, by examining their levels of commitment to cessation. Thus they found that those who were in the most need of continuing treatment for cessation, were those with both high levels of addiction rates and lower levels of commitment (Pierce 4). These studies were found to have the same rates of cessation, among all of the levels of addiction, only upon completion of a prescribed cessation plan. Whether the respondents were higher on the addiction scale or lower, they all seemed to do better with whole completion of treatments.

The next study examined was also found in the ProQuest site, as well as meeting all afore mentioned criteria. This study was taken from abstracts given from the Journal of General Internal Medicine. They looked at a particular patient, who had presented with a severe loss of breath (Abstract 1). Originally, they had considered that the symptoms were simply caused by the patients smoking history. However upon the treatment failure they began to look for other causes and found that the cause seemed to be ground up glass. The amount of ground glass seemed to be due to the level of addiction at which the patient was presently at (Abstract 3). The ground glass it would seem came from the cigarette filter, over the years it had built up. The patient has since completed cessation, as well as other treatments and is recovering quite well (Abstract 4). The reason for including this research is to show the different levels of addiction, that still have higher cessation rates. Even though this case was not typical of smokers who are trying to quit, it does show the extreme level of addiction, with the successful cessation upon completion of treatment.

The final study looked at was one which looked at the rates of smoking cessation associated with those who also have Post Traumatic Stress Disorder (McFall 1). The reason for looking at this study was to see if a disorder may have any effect on a smoker's chance of full cessation. Another reason for including this research is to see if there are any other correlations between the results from the Pierce study and this one.

This is shown by McFall when he describes his reasoning as such;

"PTSD is associated with a smoking quit rate of only 23% (5), about half that of lifetime smokers without a mental disorder (12), and falls third from the bottom in a ranking of quit rates for 13 mental disorders (5). Smokers with PTSD also experience nicotine withdrawal symptoms in response to encounters with trauma-related stimuli (13) and report smoking in order to relieve anxiety and tension (8). Taken together, this research suggests a dynamic relationship between PTSD and tobacco use that argues for a coordinated approach to the treatment of both disorders" (McFall et al 1).

This shows that both those with PTSD, as well as those without, benefit from a more integrated and complete approach to smoking cessation. In this study McFall found that the more integrated the treatment was, the better the success rates of actual cessation (McFall 2). This was the same conclusion which all the studies examined came to. This leads us to believe that not only is more research needed, but of all the research given, the conclusions are very similar. That those who have a high addiction to tobacco, for extended periods of time, can and will benefit from an integrated continuum based treatment for quitting smoking. This is also evident in studies done for those above the age of thirty-five, yet we can assume that if this approach works for those who have high rates, as well as other criteria, then it should work for those in this age bracket as well.

A Discussion on Feminism, Motherhood and the Workplace

In the text, the section on Human Nature is particularly compelling to me, as the concept of women's subjugation to men being based on the Christian creation narrative is of special concern (Boss 386). In this narrative the idea is that women are naturally subservient to man due to the creation of woman from man's rib. This is a contention for me, as in my own opinion this would prove women to be equal from this moment. In other words if they were both created from the same product of the rib's host, then they would be made in equal amounts from the same materials, thus any argument for inequality on this basis would then be insufficient. The inequality of women in my eyes is morally wrong. My reasoning for this is much the same as many others, in that humans are created with right reason, which is not subject to man's own created structural differentials. In other words, there is no difference in the innate abilities of humans to discover right reason, nor is there any difference in using said reason to guide them through their lives. All of the structural differences in societies are constructed by previous societies where men were considered to be in control of nature and every aspect therein.

However, this was also based on ideas and scientific evidence from ancient times and is safe to say that much of this early ideal has been proven wrong. Therefore, it should not still be the basis for a modern ideal. In simpler terms, gender inequality is an antiquated structural separation of work and should have no place in the 21st century. If we can send man-made objects to the farthest reaches of the cosmos, we should be able to have true equality for all humans here on this planet.

30 January 2014

The Napoleon Issue

Based on the instructions and letters from Napoleon Bonaparte, I have found that there are many factors which made his efforts successful. One of the larger reasons would have to be his use of some of the ideals from the revolution, while still retaining a monarchical position of power. The ways in which he was able to garner the respect of the people to some degree, by keeping some of the gains made by the Republic, were crucial in advancing his own ambitions for power. This coupled with his loyalty within the military, created a monstrous force to be reckoned with in Europe. In his instructions to his family members, he outlines some of these very points, in order to reinforce his Imperial vision.

One part of that vision is the control of the people whom you intend to rule. One way to achieve this is to ingratiate yourself with your subjects. Napoleon was very instrumental in doing this in the nations which he conquered. This is evident in Napoleon's letter to his stepson Eugene Beauharnais, whom he placed in Italy, in 1805.

In his instruction, he attempts to impart the importance of getting the people on your side, in this excerpt from the letter; we can see how much Napoleon believes this a matter of importance;

The purpose of your administration being the welfare of my Italian subjects, you must begin by sacrificing your prejudices against those customs of theirs which you resent so violently (1). He goes on to reiterate this point, over and over again throughout the letter. What his intention is with this type of governing advice, is to get the people on your side, you must be much more like them and much less French. Although this may not always work, it is a much better tactic than say, moving an army to the field, or having to put down an insurrection. This is one of the most important factors though in Napoleon's empire, to gain the respect of those in the populace of the country, you are better able to create an atmosphere where your rule becomes less questioned.

Another of his more effective administrative ploys is by using a military force to make his intentions clear. This could be argued to be one of the most important tactics to Napoleon's Imperial rule. This is not just about the ability to conquer by military force, but also about a continued presence, as well as everlasting devotion of the army itself. This is rather evident in his 1809 letter to his brother Jerome, where he emphasizes the real importance of having the military on your side;

> "You must be Soldier, and again a Soldier, and nothing but a Soldier" (1).

In this, Napoleon is trying to stress to his brother that being the brother of the Emperor and King, is simply not enough to garner the love of the army. One must act as a soldier, but more importantly one must be amongst his soldiers, in order to be respected by them. In this way the military is loyal and respects the commands of the king. This point is also discussed in Napoleon's letter to his brother Joseph, whom sat upon the throne of Spain. In this letter he discusses the importance of putting down insurrection, in order to keep the populace in line with the new regime. In the letter, Napoleon goes into some detail to describe how his brother must put down the insurrections and remind the populace who is in control, by appealing to their sense of security.

The rabble loves and esteems only those it fears, and only if you make yourself feared by the rabble can you make yourself loved and esteemed by the whole nation" (1).

In this, Napoleon is showing how by putting down the insurrection you will in turn become the law of the land, so to speak. In other words, if they fear being the object of your law, they will no doubt, learn to follow it without question. This is very much a traditional tactic for dealing with insurrection.

Dear Professor,

The assignment which I chose to focus on is from question number 4, on the analytical list. I chose to focus on the work of Confucius and his model of a good leader, by comparing the character of the King from the Sakuntala story, to show how the character of the King, is in line with Confucius' ideas of a good ruler. I do not think that my views of either work were changed, by writing this particular essay. However, I believe that this is due to my experiences with the works of Confucius. I also think that it could be partly due my enjoying the Sakuntala story itself, as I see the good nature of the characters within it. I think that the hardest aspect of the writing process in this essay was to be able to construct a viewable comparison between the King and Confucius's model. This was very difficult, as I did not want to lose the reader in some bit by bit analytics, but have them be able to easily draw the comparison on their own. I believe that this helped to enhance my conclusions, as well as the body of the essay by making the overall context more flowing and thus more easily read. The thesis of this essay was another bit of contention for me. I did not want to overdo it with some technical statement, which probably would not make any sense and I also wanted it to be a clear, debatable comparison. I think that I was able to achieve this, but it may still be one of the weakest parts of the essay. I have spent many years, simply reading material for its knowledge alone, so sometimes I can over analyze, or over simplify a work. I would really appreciate any feedback on this, as I would like to be able to properly interpret a piece, without overdoing it. Any kind of pointers on my grammar would also be greatly appreciated.

Sincerely,

Corey Oakes

28 February 2014

A Look at Confucius's Hindu King

The works of Confucius have long been applied to people in leadership positions throughout history. I had thought of doing exactly that, in comparing the character from the Sakuntala story, but have instead decided to examine the models which are used to show the character of a good leader. I believe that by comparing these two models from different cultures, we will see that they are indeed very similar. I will therefore, compare not just the character, but the positions of the ideal models as well. In this way, I believe that I can effectively show the various similarities between the ideal king of "Sakuntala" and the model of a good leader presented by Confucius (Silva).

Then let us begin by looking at Confucius and his "Doctrine of the Mean" (Confucius 302). What is Confucius's model of a good leader? Well first we must find his descriptions of what is right and good, and then maybe we will find what he would consider to be good leader with those qualities. In the Doctrine of the Mean, there is a passage which states Confucius's view on ones place within society. In this description he describes being content with ones given station in life, as a quality of good character, which he describes in this passage; "The superior man does what is proper to the station in which he is; he does not desire to go beyond this" (Confucius 304).

In this, I believe that he showing that to be content with ones station in life, is to be what you are and not try to be something you are not. This is consistent with the version of the king in the Sakuntala, as we can see when we look at the descriptions of the character himself. In one decision where the king's character is attempting to figure out how to explain his presence in such a place and describes it thusly;

"How now shall I reply? Shall I make myself known, or shall I still disguise my real rank? I have it; I will answer her thus. I am the person charged by his Majesty, the descendant of Puru, with the administration of justice and religion; and am come to this sacred grove to satisfy myself that the rites of the hermits are free from obstruction" (Sakuntala 387).

In this he describes his station in the caste system as an essential consideration when making any types of decision in his culture. This is a very similar position to Confucius's version and they both represent traits of character, which is essential in both readings. This is evident in The Doctrine of the Mean, as Confucius has a passage here as well in which he describes the need for consideration of one's character.

> "He who knows these three things knows how to cultivate his own character. Knowing how to cultivate his own character, he knows how to govern other men. Knowing how to govern other men, he knows how to govern the kingdom with all its states and families" (Confucius 307).

Again we are able to find this same theme in the Sakuntala story, as we look to the piece of the story where the king has regained his memory. After finding himself in error for the wrongs he had committed against his beloved Sakuntala. While in the midst of reproaching himself, he is told by a great sage that it was not his fault, as he is of good character and was not responsible considering he had lost his memory. Upon this realization he replies;

> "Oh! What a weight is taken off my mind, now that my character is cleared of reproach" (Sakuntala 478).

This clearly shows that one's character is of great importance in this cultural tale. Therefore both works seem to have at least these two characteristics of one's cultural position and one's character, but are these the only similarities?

In fact, I have found a few more similarities and it is one which would not at first seem to be, religious devotion to virtuous acts. In this I mean that they both use the path of the righteous to show how the actions of a good person or ruler will indeed lead them to a heaven where the proper characteristics are rewarded. In Confucius's work, we find that the path of the Mean is truly the path to heaven; however we are given the added pleasure of getting pretty much all of the other virtues which are important to the good leader. Here he is describing the path and the qualities which one should possess in order to lead;

"It is only he, possessed of all sagely qualities that can exist under heaven, who shows himself quick in apprehension, clear in discernment, of far-reaching intelligence, and all-embracing knowledge, fitted to exercise rule; magnanimous, generous, benign, and mild, fitted to exercise forbearance; impulsive, energetic, firm, and enduring, fitted to maintain a firm hold; self-adjusted, grave, never swerving from the Mean, and correct, fitted to command reverence; accomplished, distinctive, concentrative, and searching, fitted to exercise discrimination" (Confucius 311).

In this we can see that the qualities which are important to a leader are quite specific, but are these same qualities exhibited in the character of the king? I would argue that indeed they are not only present in the characterization of the king, but throughout the entirety of the story itself. Let us examine this statement for a moment. Does the story show us characters which are dishonest? No it only gives us characters who are the embodiment of the very qualities described by Confucius. In fact the characters are even punished for neglecting their duties within the culture, which as was stated in the first quote from Confucius is of vital importance to one's character. Does the character of the king possess any of these qualities? Well in fact he does, as was previously described in earlier quotes, he is very conscience of the value of his character, as well as being dutiful in his given social position.

Thus, combined these positions seem very similar to the description by Confucius, as well as in the benediction at the beginning of the Sakuntala. I would conclude then, that many elements of these two models are very similar, including the values which Confucius stated were of great importance for one who would rule. The Sakuntala presents characters, especially Sakuntala and the King, who are as devoted to their duties as they are righteous. They are committed to their given castes in life, yet given to more human qualities as well. They are devoted to their spirituality and very conscious of their actions. These are also the very qualities which Confucius would say are essential to being a good and just ruler, thus I see only minor differences in the works core messages. I would also say that these are both works which were meant to be guides for ways of living which are virtuous and of good a nature. Therefore both are somewhat rooted in the same ideals which both consider the ideal model for a ruler.

I hope you have enjoyed our look at the characters of these two enlightened works. I also hope that you are intrigued enough by these claims, to explore these works for yourself from this point of view.

30 April, 2015

Capital Punishment: A Moral Perspective

The moral issues associated with capital punishment are not always just the issues associated with putting someone to death. They may also include the how question, or in other words the morality in regards to how the punishment is carried out. Abolitionist arguments in fact look to the "cruel and unusual," punishments clause in the United States Constitution, as a basis for the abolition. Although this is a compelling way to frame the entirety of the issue, it does not answer the question of the overall morality of capital punishment, nor does it answer the unequal distribution of the punishment.

The answer then comes in two parts, one the morality of the issue of capital punishment itself. Once this is satisfactorily answered, then the answer comes to the equal distribution of the punishment. It is often difficult to find one single ethical answer to these, as such one must look to the area which best answers these to the examiner himself/herself. The theories which answer this and many other questions for me would be those of Natural Law developed by John Locke and The Scottish School of Common Sense. My reasoning for this is that the theories provide a platform of what they refer to as "right reason," which is the scientific component of Natural Law theories, which allows us to develop the ideas of justice by looking to whether these conform to the ideal of right reason (Boss 64-65, 2013).

In the text we find John Locke's version of the "right reason," in:

"The state of nature has a law of nature to govern it, which obliges everyone; and reason, which is that law ..." (Boss 65, 2013).

This phrase helps to give the framework for the question of, is capital punishment moral, as it shows that reason would suggest that the taking of life by one is in fact morally wrong, thus to punish one in accordance by prescribing the same like punishment would then balance the inequality of the law of nature. In other words to take another person's right to life, liberty or health, is to forfeit one's own right to life, liberty and health (Boss 65, 2013).

Therefore, I would conclude that it is in fact moral to take another's life in punishment for taking a person's life, as "right reason," would suggest that to balance the inequalities of nature; the state has the responsibility to do this for the community. As the state has become the individual in respect to the distribution of justice meant to balance the laws of nature. It has also been bestowed the responsibility of community justice, which also uses this logic to balance the safety of the community. This is not to suggest that other avenues of punishment do not need to be applied prior to coming to this most regrettable of punishments. It is only to say that the punishment seems to be moral as a balancing tool for natural law theories. It also would seem that just as Ernest Van Den Haag concluded in his defense of capital punishment, that this answer does not answer the equality of distribution question (Boss 235, 2013).

For the answer to the question of equal distribution, one must look to the reasoning behind the inequalities. In this case reason suggests that this is due to social constructs of justice within the given community. This is to say that in order to find the reasoning behind the distribution of capital punishment within a given community; one must look to the "right reason," behind the community's value of justice, as well as the social constructs of what constitutes that community. Therefore, I feel that this leaves the question of equal distribution open to communal interpretation, as each autonomous communal entity, will invariably interpret the value of justice differently.

20 March 2011

Prison Tattoos: Some of Their Meanings

I want to suggest that it would be a mistake to speak of all

prison tattoos as if they were the same (McCarron). Many prisoners'

tattoos are a narrative of their story (McCarron).   How do prison

gangs communicate using tattoos, and why do they use the different

symbolism?

In the prison system or "Gulags", prisoners are marked by

specific hierarchy system. Some examples are; the head "Thieves in

Law" are marked by a crucifixion. Next are the lesser ranking

"Thieves", who have the right to wear predatory animals such as,

tigers, and lynx (Lambert). Stars on the shoulder are another sign of

a "Thief" (Lambert). The killers for hire are marked by a dagger

piercing the skin (Lambert). Then there are the tattoos that are made

against the wearer's will. Obscene tattoos on men were often

tattooed forcibly on passive homosexuals, or people that lost at

cards. Worse still is a seemingly innocuous heart inside a white

triangle (the sign of a child rapist). Bearing this meant being an untouchable, and subject to the sexual whims of other prisoners (Hodgekinson 2). This leads me to the lowest of the low, The "Downcast", denoted by their tattoos of submissive women in a state of undress, or by eyes tattooed above the genitalia (Lambert). This is how the hierarchy works within the Russian prison systems.

The number of years however is told in Russian cupolas, meaning that the number of cupolas equals the number of years incarcerated (Lambert). In effect, the tattoos formed a service record of the criminal's transgressions. Skulls denoted a criminal authority. A cat represented a thief. On a woman, a tattoo of a penis was the kite-mark of a prostitute. Crosses on the knuckles denoted the number of times a wearer had been to prison, and a shoulder insignia marked solitary confinement (Hodgekinson).

While these tattoos have meaning within the Russian prison community, tattoos in general are seen by the outside, and the court systems, as a negative stereotype of criminal behavior (Lambert). It is clearly, at the very least, an interesting irony that when the State loses the power to tattoo those it judged to be criminals; the criminals began to tattoo themselves (McCarron).

Tattooing is illegal in prison, so prisoners use various ways to make ink, and machines (Hodgekinson). A soviet way to make ink is to melt down boot heels and mixing this with blood and urine (Hodgekinson). In the United States the most widely used method is using graphite from pencils, mixed with toothpaste and water. Also in the United States, the machines are generally made from; a fan motor connected to a toothbrush with a wire for a needle. A less mechanical method,

"Known as tebori, is the process of using needles attached to a bamboo handle and repeatedly tapping the skin in a uniform way is another way of applying tattoos. This process is generally used by the Yakuza of Japan" (Gay and Whittington).

In the United States there are many different gangs, and are prevalent in all prisons. One of the most prevalent gangs in the United States prisons is the white supremacist group, The Aryan Brotherhood. They can be identified by various tattoos such as; "White Power", or the letters A.B., these are usually accompanied by lightning bolts similar to those found on the uniforms of the Nazi S.S. (Gay and Whittington). They also use other Nazi imagery such as; the swastika, and the iron cross. Some even use Norse and Viking imagery like Viking ships, or letters of the Futhark as well. One of the next largest groups in United States prisons are the Latino Gangs, they can generally be identified by a city or street name such as; Culver city, or LA, and Broadway, or Thirteenth street, etc. These are generally accompanied by numbers or geographic names such as; south side, or west side (Gay and Whittington). Some other gangs are identifiable as well such as those with words like "Bloods" or "V.L." for Vice Lords, and numbers such as, "Rollin 90's Crips", etc. One which is considered the fastest growing gang in the world by many, not just those in prison, is "MS13" (Gay and Whittington).

This emigrated up from Central America to the United States, through the prison systems. After they were already here in the United States, but rounded up before they became MS13, and sent back to Central America, thereby creating what we know today as MS13.

In the United States prison system, the amount of time incarcerated is shown in a few different types of tattoos. One type is the use of bars, or the number of bars, equals the number of years incarcerated. Then there is the use of spider webs, this can differ slightly according to placement on the body. For instance if the web is placed on the shoulder, it is the number of years incarcerated. If they are on the elbow, then it is the number of circles in the web, equals the number of years incarcerated. Some prisoners use a simple tally mark on their chest, or sides. Tally marks are also used to show either how many informants known as "rats"; one has dealt with in their criminal career.

By acquiring his tattoos during his incarceration, then a prisoner makes concrete his identity as a convict, and that stigmatized identity carries with him to the outside world once he is released (DeMello). An example of this would be, the dragon, which can either mean power, and superiority, or it can be associated with drug addiction. Another example would be the use of the wasp piercing the skin to denote drug addiction as well. Other types of communication are symbols such as, death with a set of scales usually meaning that, that person has committed a murder. A set of scales by themselves says that person is a drug dealer. The S.S. Tattoos mentioned earlier are also a symbol of committing a murder, or a severe hate crime (Gay and Whittington). A criminal with no tattoos is devoid of status, but to have a tattoo when you haven't earned it is usually removed forcibly (Hodgekinson). Some even show there disregard for the establishment by getting tattoos of the "Cheshire" grin, or the letters F.T.P. (Hodgekinson).

"A lot of these guys knew they would never be released from prison, so they could not care less what the authorities did to them" (Hodgekinson).

In my experiences inside the walls, tattoos are way to show where your loyalties lie. One way to show this is by getting "Member" tattoos such as, the Aryan Brotherhood tattoos, A.B., White Power, or the Latino West Side, MS13, or some other inside affiliation. However, there are also other groups within the prisons which use tattoos as membership as well. Some examples of which would be, the use of the Four Directions symbol used by the Native Americans to denote membership, they may also use the individual tribe names as well. The use of the letters F.T.W., to denote membership with the "Pecker-woods", or whites is another example. There are many different variations within the prison system, but these are fairly common throughout. Communicating on the outside is integral as well. Tattoos used to do so are thing such as a girlfriend or wife getting tattooed with certain plants, or flowers in certain areas of the body, like the ankles. These would communicate drug shipments, and transactions occurring during visits.

In conclusion people no matter where they are have the need to communicate. In prison system they have, and will continue to use tattoos as a means of communicating who they are, and what they have done. Some will use them to coordinate drug transactions, and some may use them to show their loyalties, yet others will use them to tell their story, but all will still use them to inevitably communicate. Though resigned to the reality of prison life, the prisoner still clings to his right to do with as he will with his own body (McCarron). The more that the authorities attempt to discover the codes, and interpretations of these tattoos, the more elaborate tattoo communications the criminal will create. The fact that more, and more people are entering our prisons every year, leads me to believe that the continued use of Tattoos as a form of communication, will not only continue, but more than likely increase, as the prison population increases. In my own experiences,

I have learned these communication rules, and styles out of necessity, however in my years since incarceration I have seen a definite increase in the understandings, and uses of these methods of communication carried to the outside world more and, more every year.

Corey Oakes

Adult Learning: Andragogy

What is Andragogy, and why do we need it?

The Encyclopedia Britannica describes adult learning as being any type of learning that is done by, or for an adult (Adult 2013). Does this really tell us all that we need to know, of course it doesn't. For a better definition, we should look at the adult, in adult learning. There are a multitude of different definitions of adult, but for our purposes, we will look at adult learners, much as we look at ourselves. After all, we are in this class, thus we are learning adults. With this very general definition in mind, we can now move on to discussing the andragogy associated with our definition.

First of all, what is andragogy, and what does it have to do with adult learning? For that, we turn to Malcolm Knowles. Christopher Pappas explains Malcolm Knowles version of andragogy, in his paper on eLearning as;

"According to Malcolm Knowles, andragogy is the art and science of adult learning" (Pappas 2013).

This description of andragogy is followed up by a description of Knowles' five assumption of adult learning. These five assumptions consist of; Self-Concept, adult learner experience, readiness to learn, orientation to learn and motivation to learn (Pappas 2013). These assumptions, seem pretty self-explanatory to me, but let us examine some of them. What does Knowles assume of adult learners? Well, it would seem that he assumes that they have developed a good self-concept of themselves, as evidenced by their participation in an adult learning environment. He also would seem to assume that the learner has past educational experiences, which will influence their educational experiences in the future. The next assumption that we see him make is concerning the learner's readiness to learn, which is to say, how ready are they to learn. Orientation to learn seems a bit different to assume, but I believe that the meaning concerns ones orientation to learning in general. Although these may only be assumptions, they can still be quite accurate.

In my own adult learning experiences, I have found that these assumptions are pretty spot on. For example, when I first started my college learning experience I was only sixteen years old and I was not successful. I do believe that the reason for this is that I was too young to really be ready for college, nor was there any motivation for me to do well. Therefore, I was busy living like a college student, but not actually being a college student. Later, when I was ready to return to school, I was much more successful. The reasons behind why people return to schooling are many, yet they all seem to be centered on bettering ones situation in life. Another reason may be simple motivation such as described by Valerie McGrath, in her paper examining Knowles Principals. She states;

"Adult learners need to know why they are learning new knowledge before they are willing to participate" (McGrath 2013).

This is where; I believe the andragogy comes into play. Let me explain, by looking to some of the basic principles of the andragogy theory, we find that they can serve quite well as guides to keep us as learners on track. First of all, if we understand that we are motivated by learning new knowledge that is somehow beneficial to us, then we can better prepare ourselves to be ready to learn. Thus, we become more oriented to learn as part of the process of preparing to be ready.

There are quite a few different theories on adult learning, most of which are very similar. The opposite theory to Andragogy is Pedagogy, which is the basic premise that adult learners will simply learn the material given to them (Pappas 2013). This seems to have been the dominant theory in education for primary school. This is quite unfortunate, as it does not really prepare the student for their future learning experiences. What of those future learning experiences, in the twenty-first century learning environment. Will these theories be able to help us as students in an online environment?

I believe that they will, in fact, I think that they will become even more relevant than they were previously. Professor Ross-Gordon of Texas State University explains how some of these issues become relevant. In her article on the Association of American Colleges and Universities website she explains;

"Reentry adults' multiple roles and commitments increase the likelihood they will look for degree and certificate programs that provide them flexibility in time and locations for both course completion and for access to key student services" (Ross-Gordon 2011).

This is fairly accurate in my experience, as it probably is for most of the other students in online universities. The flexibility of the online schools, offer an accessible option for those who otherwise would not be able to attend a school. This is only going to increase as we get farther in to the twenty-first century, and thus the andragogy will become much more applicable as we move forward. The pedagogy theory, will not be able to keep up with all of the different types of adult learners entering the schools, thus the andragogy theory will probably simply evolve as the needs of the adult learners evolve.

The reasons for needing to know what andragogy is and why we will need it are around us daily, from every day chores to the children. If we are to be successful students, I believe that the andragogy, and the theories associated with it are going to be ever more important in our continuing educational endeavors, as we will need to keep in mind, what our goals are. I do hope that I have given some idea of what andragogy is, and why we must examine the

principals behind it.

Bibliography

My Social Reference

BBC. Scottish Independence Referendum Debate. (2014). Minutes 11:04-11:12. Retrieved from:

http://www.youtube.com/watch?v=jNeWvU1UQdQ

Q&A 1 References

1. Bach, Stephen. "IRLS 210 D007 Win14: Lessons." Charles Town, WV: APUS. Weeks 4-6.

https://edge.apus.edu/portal/site/246728/page/a5e7e531-e6f0-4133-a971-4612efb9963e

2. BBC. 2014. Geography: GCSE Bitesize. "Globalization." UK: British Broadcasting Company. p1-5.

http://www.bbc.co.uk/schools/gcsebitesize/geography/globalisation/globalisation_rev1.shtml

3. Cragg, Wesley, Denis Arnold, and Peter Muchlinski. 2012. "Human Rights and Business." Business Ethics Quarterly 22 (1) (January): 1–7.

4. EL-Erian, Mohamed A. "The Political Economy of 2013." 2013.

Project Syndicate (January): 1. http://www.project-

syndicate.org/commentary/how-politics-will-drive-economic-

performance-in-2013-by-mohamed-a--el-

erian#DDx66hLHfvlojjFP.99

Q&A 2 References

Global Policy Forum. "Globalization of the Economy." 2005-2013.

(n.a) gpf@globalpolicy.org. Accessed; November 30, 2013. Web.

http://www.globalpolicy.org/globalization/globalization-of-the-

economy-2-1.html

Hogan, K., Lesson 7: Public Policy. Politics 210.APUS.edu.

Accessed. November 30, 2013.Web.

Q&A 3 References

Arquilla, John. 2007. "Of Networks and Nations." The Brown

Journal of World Affairs XIV (1): 199–209. Accessed on 24 April,

2014.

http://web.b.ebscohost.com.ezproxy1.apus.edu/ehost/pdfviewer/pdfv
iewer?sid=dd7b3cad-95cb-4e2c-9819-
6a7e7336f313%40sessionmgr113&vid=2&hid=121

Bach, Stephen. 2014. "Week Seven: Network Actors (Terrorists and other Non-State Actors)." Charlestown, West Virginia: APUS IRLS210.

https://edge.apus.edu/portal/site/246728/page/a5e7e531-e6f0-4133-a971-4612efb9963e

Kellogg, David. 2010. "Crisis Guide: Pakistan." cfr.org. Accessed on 26 April, 2014.

http://www.cfr.org/interactives/CG_Pakistan/index.html

Kerry, John. "Trafficking in Persons Report: Remarks at the Annual Meeting of the President's Interagency Task Force To Monitor and Combat Trafficking in Persons." 2013. US Dept. of State. Washington, D.C. Accessed on 22 April, 2014.

http://www.state.gov/secretary/remarks/2014/04/224655.htm

Weimann, Gabriel. 2010. "Terror on Facebook, Twitter, and YouTube." Brown Journal of World Affairs XVI (II): 45–54. Accessed on 21 April, 2014.

http://web.a.ebscohost.com.ezproxy1.apus.edu/ehost/pdfviewer/pdfviewer?sid=e4729855-2b4f-4542-86b1-5c42117027cd%40sessionmgr4001&vid=2&hid=4101

Excerpts Bibliography

Jernigan, Kelly, editor. "Excerpts from the Treaty of Versailles, 28 June 1919." Provided in HIST122 D2 Sum 2011 at American Public University Systems.

Hunt, Lynn, et. al. *The Making of The West: Peoples and Cultures, Vol. 2: Since 1500. 3rd Ed.* Boston, MA: Bedford/St. Martins, 2009.

Structural Reference

The United Nations and Civil Society: Report of the Thirtieth UN Issues Conference. (1999). Web. Retrieved from:

http://www.globalpolicy.org/component/content/article/177/31816.html

Three Favorites References

Fukuyama, Francis. 1989. The end of history. National Interest, no. 16 (Summer): 178-182.

URL: http://ps321.community.uaf.edu/files/2012/10/Fukuyama-End-of-history-article.pdf

Kaufman, Stuart. 1997. The fragmentation and consolidation of international systems.

International Organization 51, no. 2 (Spring): 173-208. (Pages 173-186 and 200-208)

URL:http://ezproxy.apus.edu/login?url=http://search.ebscohost.com/login.aspx?direct=true&db=tsh&AN=9706050282&site=ehost-live

Tin-bor Hui, Victoria. 2004. Toward a dynamic theory of international politics: Insights from

comparing ancient China and early modern Europe. International Organization 58 (Winter): 175-205.

http://web.b.ebscohost.com.ezproxy2.apus.edu/ehost/pdfviewer/pdfv
iewer?sid=4b0b65c9-d4a3-4991-b2f2-
019b200e0328%40sessionmgr110&vid=2&hid=112

General Foreign Policy References

Rosati, Jerel A. and James M. Scott. 2011. The Politics of United
States Foreign Policy. 5th ed. Independence, KY: Wadsworth
Publishing. Retrieved From:

http://ebooks.apus.edu.ezproxy2.apus.edu/IRLS214/Rosati_2
011_Ch01.pdf

Rosati, Jerel A. and James M. Scott. 2011. The Politics of United
States Foreign Policy. 5th ed. Independence, KY: Wadsworth
Publishing. Retrieved From:

http://ebooks.apus.edu.ezproxy2.apus.edu/IRLS214/Rosati_2011_Ch
02.pdf

Rosati, Jerel A. and James M. Scott. 2011. The Politics of United
States Foreign Policy. 5th ed. Independence, KY: Wadsworth
Publishing. Retrieved From:

138

http://ebooks.apus.edu.ezproxy2.apus.edu/IRLS214/Rosati_2011_Ch03.pdf

Grimmett, Richard F. U.S. Department of State, Foreign Affairs and National Defense Division. June 1, 1999 "Foreign Policy Roles of the President and Congress." 16 November, 2015. Web.

http://fpc.state.gov/6172.htm

Palestinian Experience Bibliography

Cainkar,Louise."Palestinians": *Encyclopedia of Chicago. 2005.* March 13 2013.www.encyclopedia.chicagohistory.org/pages/946.html

Carter, Jimmy. "Palestine Peace Not Apartheid". *Simon &Schuster* New York, NY. 2006. Print.

Cohen, Yinon and Andrea Tyree. "Palestinian and Jewish Israeli-Born Immigrants in the United States": *International Migration Review: The Center for Migration Studies of New York.* 1994. Web. March 13 2013. www.jstor.org/MonJul 29 15:36:51 2002.

Ibish,Hussein. "Palestinians in the United States: The Untold

Success Story". *This week in Palestine.* March 2008. Web. March 13

2013.

www.thisweekinpalestine.com/details.php?id=24108&ed=151&edid

=151

Healey, Joseph F. "Diversity and Society":Race, Ethnicity, and

Gender". *Pine Forge Press.* 2010. Print.

Classism Works Cited

1. Class Action. "About Class." Jamaica Plain, MA: Classism.org,
2004. Web. Accessed on 7 July, 2015.

http://www.classism.org/about-class/

2. Kozol, Jonothan. *Still Separate, Still Unequal America: America's
Educational Apartheid.* New York: Harper's Magazine v.311,
n.1864, 2005. Web. Accessed on 7 July, 2015.

http://www.mindfully.org/Reform/2005/American-Apartheid-
Education1sep05.htm

3. Myers, Lora. *People Like Us: Social Class in America: Teacher's
Guide.* New York: The Center for New American Media, 2001.
Web. Accessed on 7 July, 2015.

http://www.cnam.com/people-like-us/resources/Teachers_Guide.pdf

4. Nazroo, James Y. *The Structuring of Ethnic Inequalities in Health: Economic Position, Racial Discrimination, and Racism.* Washington D.C.: American Journal of Public Health: Vol 93, No. 2, 2003. Web. Accessed on 7 July, 2015.
http://ajph.aphapublications.org/doi/pdf/10.2105/AJPH.93.2.277

5. Saxton, Alexander. *The Rise and Fall of the White Republic: Class Politics and Mass Culture in the United States.* New York: Verso, 2003. Web. Accessed on 7 July, 2015.

https://books.google.com/books?hl=en&lr=&id=GiAJEtgCQ9UC&oi=fnd&pg=PR11&dq=current+class+differentials+in+the+United+States+economic+and+cultural+disparities&ots=x0lQI7uOrX&sig=nAG5XO_4SeLKkNHYmcETAJsZ8Go#v=onepage&q=current%20class%20differentials%20in%20the%20United%20States%20economic%20and%20cultural%20disparities&f=false

6. Scott, Janny and David Leonhardt. "Shadowy Lines That Still Divide." New York: New York Times, 2005. Web. Accessed on 7 July, 2015.

http://www.nytimes.com/2005/05/15/us/class/shadowy-lines-that-still-divide.html

Historical Law Reference

The Cherokee Nation v. The State of Georgia, 30 US 1 - Supreme

Court 1831

Google Scholar.Web.Accessed November 30, 2013.

http://scholar.google.com/scholar_case?case=648152410090361190

9&q=Cherokee+Nation+v.+Georgia+(1831)&hl=en&as_sdt=3,48

Smoking Cessation Works Cited

"Abstracts from the 31st Annual Meeting of the Society of General

Internal Medicine." *Journal of General Internal Medicine* 23

(2008): 89-443. *ProQuest.* Web. 30 Oct. 2013.

McFall, Miles, et al. "Improving the Rates of Quitting Smoking for

Veterans with Posttraumatic Stress Disorder." The American Journal

of Psychiatry 162.7 (2005): 1311-9. ProQuest. Web. 23 Oct. 2013.

Pierce, John P., Arthur J. Farkas, and Elizabeth A. Gilpin. "Beyond

Stages of Change: The Quitting Continuum Measures Progress

Towards Successful Smoking Cessation." *Addiction* 93.2 (1998):

277-86. *ProQuest.* Web. 23 Oct. 2013.

Feminism Reference

Boss, Judith A. *Analyzing Moral Issues: Sixth Edition.* New York:

Boss, 2013. Print.

Napoleon Issue Work Cited

Bonaparte, Napoleon. "Instructions and Letters, 1805-1809."

Reproduced by J. Christopher Harold, editor and translator. *The*

Mind of Napoleon: A Selection from His Written and Spoken Words.

New York: Columbia University Press, 1955.

Confucius Works Cited

Confucius, *The Doctrine of The Mean,* Ed., Silva, Linda and William

Overton. *World Literature Anthology: Through the Renaissance.*

Vol.2, Charles Town, WV: APUS E-Press, 2011. Web. Accessed on

25 February, 2014.

Kalidasa. *The Sakuntala*, trans, Monier Monier-Williams. Ed. Silva,

Linda and William Overton. *World Literature Anthology: Through*

the Renaissance. Vol.2, Charles Town, WV: APUS E-Press, 2011.

Web. Accessed on 25 February, 2014.

Silva, Linda and William Overton. *World Literature Anthology: Through the Renaissance.* Vol.2, Charles Town, WV: APUS E-Press, 2011. Web. Accessed on 25 February, 2014.

Capital Punishment Reference

1. Judith A. Boss, *Analyzing Moral Issues: Sixth Edition* (New York: McGraw-Hill, 2013), 64-235.

Andragogy References

Adult Learning. (2013). In Encyclopedia Britannica Online. Sept. 28 2013. Retrieved From

http://www.britannica.com/EBchecked/topic/6610/adult-education

McGrath, V. (n.d.) Reviewing the Evidence on How Adult Students Learn: An Examination of Knowles' Model of Andragogy. Cleveland Memberlodge (n.d.). p 99-110. Retrieved from;

http://astdcleveland.memberlodge.com/Resources/Documents/andragogy.pdf

Pappas, C. (n.d). Adult Learning Theory-of Malcolm Knowles. elearning industry. Sept. 28 2013. Retrieved from http://elearningindustry.com/the-adult-learning-theory-andragogy-of-malcolm-knowles

Ross-Gordon, J.M. (2011). Research on Adult Learners: Supporting the Needs of a Student Population that is No Longer Nontraditional, Vol. 13 (issue 1). Sept. 28 2013. Retrieved from http://aacu.org/peerreview/pr-wi11/prwi11_rossgordon.cfm

www.ingramcontent.com/pod-product-compliance
Lightning Source LLC
Chambersburg PA
CBHW071404280526
45787CB00001B/424